What people are saying about *The Politically Incorrect Wife* (formerly *Is There a Moose in Your Marriage?*)

"As our marriages and our homes disintegrate, we often point our finger at others to assign blame. It is refreshing to read *The Politically Incorrect Wife*, which is focused on our own responsibility to be who God has called us to be. Three cheers for Nancy Cobb and Connie Grigsby! Their book gives more than just answers; it gives truth and hope. It is a book that I look forward to sharing with my own daughters."

ANNE GRAHAM LOTZ, SPEAKER AND AUTHOR OF *JUST GIVE ME JESUS*

"Practical, fun, and absolutely life changing. You'll laugh, but you will also be inspired. It's perfect for newlyweds, but also for those, like me, who have been married a long time and have wonderful marriages. I can't recommend this manual for wives from Nancy Cobb and Connie Grigsby highly enough."

DEE BRESTIN, SPEAKER AND AUTHOR OF *THE FRIENDSHIPS OF WOMEN*

"As a result of The Wife Class [based on material in this book], the women of our church have a clearer understanding of God's design for them in their role as wives. As they begin to live accordingly, they reap the benefits of personal peace and new harmony in their marriages."

ROBERT L. THUNE, SENIOR PASTOR,
OMAHA, NEBRASKA

"The many "how to's" found within *The Politically Incorrect Wife* will show you how to gently unwrap the gift that is your mate! We've been blessed to read most of the current books on marriage, and this is one of the very best!"

BOB AND DIANE REILLY, MARRIAGE MINISTRIES INTERNATIONAL,
COHOSTS OF *MARRIAGE MATTERS*

"*The Politically Incorrect Wife* is a must-have book for every pastor's library. Nancy and Connie's sound biblical teaching and Spirit-filled insights can benefit every pastor engaged in premarital and marriage counseling."

REVEREND KENNETH LETTERMAN, FAITH PRESBYTERIAN CHURCH, GERMANTOWN, TENNESSEE

"What gives this book credibility are the transformed marriages in our church because of these authors' lives, teaching, and mentoring. This is required reading for women who long for a more fulfilling marriage."

PASTOR WENDELL NELSON

"I am the recipient and blessed husband of a wife who applied (and still does) the principles enumerated in this excellent and very practical book. They have marvelously changed my life on this earth and for eternity."

LARRY WRIGHT, FOUNDER, ABUNDANT LIFE, INC.

"Get out your highlighter and read this book...you won't be disappointed!"

KENT JULIAN, NATIONAL DIRECTOR OF ALLIANCE YOUTH

And now, *How to Get Your Husband to Talk to You:*

"Don't miss this book! It's fun, realistic, smart, helpful—on every page. Mind you, I don't have any *feelings* about it. We're talking straight problem-solving here…. Think of it as an armchair travel book, an interplanetary cruise, a Grunt-English dictionary. Think of it as 'your husband is a TV,' and you—for once—have the remote."

DAVID KOPP, COAUTHOR WITH HEATHER HARPHAM-KOPP, OF
LOVE STORIES GOD TOLD AND *PRAYING THE BIBLE FOR YOUR MARRIAGE*

"Nancy and Connie have filled this book with wise and wonderful counsel on understanding the differences between how men and women communicate. *How to Get Your Husband to Talk to You* is a treasure of personal experiences, tried and true ideas, and seasoned insights on marriage. My husband and I have been married almost 44 years, and how I wish I'd had this book in the early years! Whether you're a new bride or have been married for many years, following the advice in this book can greatly improve your marriage. You may even fall in love with your husband all over again!"

SHEILA CRAGG, CREATOR OF WWW.WOMANSWALK.COM

"*How to Get Your Husband to Talk to You* addresses an age-old question asked by all women in love. Connie and Nancy offer a fresh reminder to honor and accept your man. You'll learn how to frame your words, diminish your details, and acknowledge your differences. The authors' warm, story-vignette style of writing makes this book an easy, quick read."

DONNA OTTO, AUTHOR OF *THE GENTLE ART OF MENTORING,*
FOUNDER OF HOMEMAKERS BY CHOICE

THE
Politically
INCORRECT
Wife

WITH STUDY GUIDE

NANCY COBB
CONNIE GRIGSBY

Multnomah Books

THE POLITICALLY INCORRECT WIFE
published by Multnomah Books
A division of Random House, Inc.

© 2000, 2002 by Nancy Cobb and Connie Grigsby
International Standard Book Number: 978-1-59052-110-6

Cover design and image by Koechel Peterson and Associates

For information:
MULTNOMAH BOOKS
12265 ORACLE BOULEVARD, SUITE 200 • COLORADO SPRINGS, CO 80921

Library of Congress Cataloging-in-Publication Data

Cobb, Nancy, 1938-
  The politically incorrect wife / Nancy Cobb and Connie Grigsby.
    p. cm.
Includes bibliographical references.
  ISBN 1-59052-110-2 (trade pbk.)
  1. Wives—Religious life. 2. Christian women—Religious life. 3. Marriage—Religious
aspects—Christianity. I. Grigsby, Connie. II. Title.

BV4528.15 C64 2003
248.8'435—dc21

                              2002013336

07 08 09 10—10 9 8 7 6

To Ray,
after all these years,
the walk grows sweeter still.
In memory of Dad,
for always showing me the
importance of loving others.
Thank you for the lesson and your love.
To Anne Graham Lotz,
my dear friend and mentor,
who over twenty years ago
introduced me to my Savior.

NANCY COBB

To Wes,
for your commitment,
your integrity,
and your love.
And to Daddy and Mom,
I wouldn't trade my
childhood for
anything in this world.
Thank you.

CONNIE GRIGSBY

Contents

PART 5: THE MOTIVE

PART 6: THE RESULTS

Acknowledgments

Thank you to Ed Condra, who from across the ocean in Papua New Guinea, answered our many questions and provided invaluable insight into the Word.

Thank you to Nancy Thompson, Renee DeLoriea, and Jennifer Gott, our wonderful editors, for polishing our rough edges and spurring us to higher thinking. We deeply value your wisdom, knowledge of God's Word, and faith in our message. We also know that without your help, this book would have been too heavy to carry!

Thank you to Multnomah Publishers for giving us the opportunity to write. We so appreciate being a part of your team.

Thank you to Suzanne Freshman, who planted the original seed to begin a work on marriage, which developed into this book.

Thank you to our families and friends for your encouragement and unwavering belief that we should write this book. Thank you for your prayers, your cheers, and your love. The finish line was sweeter because of you.

Most of all, thanks be to God. We love You, Lord, and give You all the glory, honor, and praise.

What Is a Politically Incorrect Wife?

*Y*ou're probably wondering that right now, aren't you? The politically incorrect wife is a woman who is married to her husband—and not married to popular American culture. How she views her husband and how she treats him are not determined by society's widely accepted ideologies. In fact, she firmly refuses to bend to mind-sets that would ultimately damage her marriage. It's not that she doesn't hold herself to a set of standards; she does. But her standards are different—higher, actually—than standards considered politically correct because they do not offend people who hold to commonly agreed-upon thought.

The politically incorrect wife *does not* buy into modern-day thinking that says:

1. You are in control of your own life.
2. Marriage is a fifty-fifty proposition.
3. You should treat your husband like he treats you.
4. Your feelings are your guide.
5. Your husband needs to earn your respect.

6. You should make him pay for your forgiveness.
7. There's no such thing as a happy marriage anymore.
8. Your husband's job is to make you happy.

The politically incorrect wife *does* hold to these spiritual principles, which transform from the inside out:

1. Doing things God's way is the key to having a joyful life.
2. I am 100 percent responsible to God for my behavior as a wife.
3. I'll love my husband unconditionally.
4. I will act the way I want to feel.
5. Respecting my husband brings glory to God.
6. Forgiveness is a choice, not a feeling.
7. A Source of power is readily available to help me!
8. My joy is not determined by another human being.

When it comes to both of these approaches to being a wife, you can be confident that we (Nancy and Connie) speak with voices of experience. Between the two of us, we bought into modern-day thinking regarding marriage for nearly forty years! During that very long and arduous time, we flowed right along with emerging cultural values and became more entrenched in the idea that our husbands had to earn their way to our hearts. Over the years we became stingier about how much love, affection, care, and concern we doled out to our husbands. In our minds, it made perfect sense for us to suspiciously measure the amount of love we thought our husbands were giving us and then treat them accordingly.

Our modus operandi was faulty for a number of reasons. For one thing, we were clueless to the fact that our measuring tools did not take into account that a man's way of showing love to a woman oftentimes does not directly correspond to how a woman perceives love. Because we were using the wrong measuring tools, we didn't realize that our husbands had been expressing their love to us all along—but from their male perspectives (imagine that!).

And we held it against them!

Of course, looking back now, it's easy to see just how selfish and self-centered our idea of love really was. It's also easy to see how our mind-sets were molded by society's present-day messages, which basically say, "I only do something for you if I can get something out of it."

Until we discovered God's plan for marriage and began to follow His set of standards, our husbands felt like they couldn't win no matter what they did.

So they stopped trying.

And so did we!

Being politically correct kept our marriages in "stuck" position for years—so much so that if you had taken a snapshot of our marriages during that time, you would have found cold hearts and unhappy husbands who were resigned to living with emotionally distant and often angry wives.

By God's grace, we discovered a life-changing truth: Political correctness doesn't work in a marriage. We were shocked to learn this! After all, we had spent years shaping our lives around this faulty view. Now, however, we consider that view to be utter foolishness and thank God every day for showing us the spiritual principles in His plan for marriage.

SHARING THE FRUIT WITH YOU

Not long after discovering God's scriptural "job description" for wives, I (Nancy) realized that if I wanted to have a passionate relationship with Christ, I needed to do what He said. Since that's what I wanted, I began being a wife God's way—a wife empowered by the very One who created marriage. This turned my world upside down! Within weeks, God changed my heart of stone into a heart of love for my husband, Ray. I now have the best of both worlds. I love the Lord with all my heart and have never loved Ray more!

For me (Connie), becoming politically incorrect in this area changed not only my marriage, but my life as well. I developed a genuine love for my husband, and I no longer treated him in an in-kind manner. This liberated him to love me in a fresh way. It softened his heart toward me beyond description. Our daughters comment on this regularly. Most of all, becoming a politically incorrect wife opened the door to an intimate relationship with God. I believe my treatment of Wes stood in the way of that for years. Why would God shower His blessings on a stony heart? He didn't! Before, I loved God in a casual sense. Now, I love Him with a passion.

After we (Nancy and Connie) met and got to know each other, we discovered that each of our lives had been radically transformed when we began to follow God's ways in the area of marriage. We also discovered that we have a similar passion for helping women develop an intimate love relationship with Jesus and walk in the freedom of having their primary ministry—their marriage—in order.

THE ROAD LESS TRAVELED

So how did we come up with the concept of the politically incorrect wife? Not long ago, we were talking with a woman who was unhappy in her marriage. She wanted to know what she could do to get her husband to change. After all, she mused, aren't husbands the ones who need changing the most?

We began to share our thoughts and ideas about what fulfills a woman in marriage. And to her amazement, it had nothing to do with changing her husband.

She grew quiet and mulled over our words for quite some time. Finally she announced, "You know, the trouble with what you're saying is that it's so *politically incorrect* to act that way."

"Certainly it is that," we agreed. "But the real problem isn't that it's politically incorrect. The problem is that political correctness simply doesn't work in a marriage."

We then challenged her to consider becoming a politically incorrect wife. She said she just didn't know if she could do it because her way made so much more sense to her.

"Tell us again how well your way is working," we responded, with a bit of amusement in our voices.

She burst into laughter! Obviously her way wasn't working at all, for her answer began with the words, "I'm so unhappy in my marriage I could die." (To say it wasn't working was a huge under-statement!)

So the woman agreed to consider changing her course. We seriously wondered if she'd forsake the familiar for the unfamiliar. However, she was so unhappy in her marriage that we thought she might.

Then, two weeks later, one of us received a call from her.

"I can't believe it," she exclaimed. "I'm happier than I've been in years. We still have a long way to go, but I feel as if a huge weight has been lifted from my shoulders. I feel like the five-hundred-pound gorilla is no longer sitting on my back. I feel like I'm becom-ing me again—I'd lost me for such a long time."

WHAT HAS BEEN LOST CAN BE FOUND

Have you lost "you"? Are you wondering where the woman your husband married went? Do you sometimes look in the mirror and wonder where that radiant bride who walked down the aisle has disappeared to? Are you tired of running in place and going nowhere in your marriage? Perhaps it's time you considered becoming a politically incorrect wife. Don't allow anything to impede your forward motion a minute longer! Allow truth to get you back on track in your marriage and in your life!

We remember again the words of our friend: "You know, the trouble with what you're saying is that it's so politically incorrect to act that way."

No, that's not the problem…that's the beauty!

Implementing the spiritual principles described in this book can help turn your marriage around too. Being politically incorrect will strengthen you and your marriage.

We're not going to tell you that living out the high calling of being a politically incorrect wife is easy. Actually, it requires tremendous strength! But you will see as you read through and apply the principles in this book that you don't have to muster up the strength to do it on your own because God will help you every step of the way.

May God shower His blessings upon you as you begin your walk down this exciting path of freedom in Christ.

Nancy Cobb and Connie Grigsby

Part One

Titles

ARE

Important

Chapter One: Men Need Help

Do you have the aptitude, the capacity, for learning how to become a godly wife? Of course you do! Have you ever wished that there was some kind of job description telling you just how to do that? There is! It was given long ago in a garden called Eden to a woman named Eve.

God's plan is far different from the world's.

It is harder. It is higher. It is holier.

His plan for marriage isn't hard. It's impossible! You can never be successful on your own. But the impossible becomes possible because of Jesus. He alone gives us the power to be who He designed us to be—godly women and wives.

Can you do it? Of course! All that's required is your willingness to follow Him.

Look to Christ…and let the changes begin in you.

Men Need Help

*The turning point in a marriage is often so small
and unheralded that you can almost miss it.*

There it was. The suitcase. Sitting at the top of the basement stairs. The very sight of it made her angry. Her
husband had just returned from a business trip and
had left the suitcase there, assuring her that very soon he would
take it downstairs and put it away.

A week later the suitcase was still there. Since the washing
machine was in the basement, she was forced to step over it time
and time again as she did the laundry. Before long, the way she
treated her husband was directly related to the number of times she
stepped over the suitcase. It was the middle of January, and outside
the temperature was dropping rapidly. Inside, it was plummeting as
well.

One day she decided to move the suitcase. No, she didn't take
it downstairs and put it away. Helping was the last thing on her
mind. Instead, she carried it into their bedroom and put it down in
the middle of the floor where her husband walked, effectively
blocking his path to the bed. Now he would see firsthand how irri-
tating it was to arrange one's life around a misplaced suitcase.

She returned to the kitchen, expecting to feel a certain amount of satisfaction and relief. She felt neither. Nor did she feel the least bit smug. What she felt was an overwhelming sense of sadness and grief. She knew her husband had not intentionally left the suitcase out; he had simply forgotten about it. Yet even knowing that, she clung to her "right" to feel offended and hostile.

She stood in the kitchen and thought about the suitcase. Had it belonged to guests, she would have happily taken it from their hands and insisted on putting it away herself. So why, she wondered, was she unwilling to help her husband in the same way? Why was it so much easier to serve others than it was to serve her husband? She took a good long look at herself and didn't like what she saw. No wonder she felt grieved. Something needed to change, all right, and it had nothing at all to do with a suitcase.

A WIFE'S CALLING IS FROM GOD

If someone asked you what the most satisfying aspect of your life is, what would you answer? Is it being a

mother?

teacher?

friend?

career woman?

grandparent?

Where would being a wife fit? Would it make the top five, or would it fall miserably toward the bottom?

For many years, our marriage relationships were the least fulfilling, least satisfying, and least successful relationships either of us experienced. Though we didn't know each other at the time, our lives were amazingly similar in this regard. We got along well with everyone else in our lives—our families, friends, neighbors, the postman, bank tellers, store clerks. Everyone except our husbands. This was troublesome and discouraging, but at some point along the way, we let ourselves off the hook by deciding that this surely must be "their problem."

But it wasn't our husbands' problem; it was ours. We had no idea what God's job description was for us as wives, so we weren't doing what we could to be the wives God wanted us to be. It was only when we discovered this job description and began applying biblical principles to our marriages that we began to find satisfaction and happiness as wives *and* as women.

God never intended for us to be frustrated or confused. He was clear and exact about our role when He stood in His freshly formed Garden. *And He hasn't changed His mind.* Popular opinion would have us believe that as the world progresses so should our thinking. But that simply isn't true in regard to God's Word. It remains the one steady thing in a constantly changing world.

GOD KNOWS OUR DIFFERENCES

In testing the market for this book, we went into a large, nationally known bookstore and asked the manager what books were available on a wife's job description.

"After scanning five hundred entries, all I can find on *wife* is listed under fiction," she said.

We told her of our plans to write such a book, and a doubtful expression crossed her face. As we left the store, she called out, "Be careful!"

We asked her what she meant.

"Every woman is so different, how can you possibly write one job description that would fit all women?"

Of course God knew just how different we are when He specifically spelled out His expectations, promises, and blessings for a woman who takes on the role of wife as He created it. Just as His Word does not change in a changing world, it does not vacillate according to our differences.

Three main points will be discussed in this chapter.

- The Role: Helper
- The Reason: Man's Aloneness
- The Relationship: Marriage

As we look at these aspects of our job description, we will see that they are perfectly designed for us by God.

THE ROLE: HELPER

God's plan for us was revealed as He put the finishing touches on His creation. It's found in Genesis 2 and is simple and straightforward:

It is not good (sufficient, satisfactory) that the man should be alone; I will make him a helper meet (suitable, adapted, complementary) for him. (v. 18, AMP)

There it is, God's perfect plan for a wife! To be a helper. God's role for a wife today is the same as it was in the Garden of Eden. Why would God create and bless all He had brought into being, from the skies and seas to the plants and trees, comment that "it is good," and then deliberately shortchange women? *He would not, and He did not.* We were called by God to a role that only we could fulfill. In God's eyes, creation was not complete without woman.

And God Created Woman

God had created the heavens and the earth and all things that existed therein and declared them to be not only good, but *very* good. Then God formed man of dust from the ground and breathed life into his nostrils, and Adam became a living being. God gave Adam the responsibility of rulership and of cultivating the Garden. He was given the freedom to eat from any tree but one. God warned him that if he did eat from the forbidden tree, he would die (Genesis 1:26–31; 2:7–8, 16–17).

Then God said that it was not good for man to be alone (2:18). Adam's *aloneness* was deemed to be "not good" by a perfect God. Have you ever thought about that? This was the first time He said that something about His creation wasn't good.

He had Adam uncover his own need by first directing him to give names to all the animals. In doing so, Adam discovered that there was no one suitable for him (vv. 19–20). Woman was then created (vv. 22–23). Many are surprised to learn that this role was given while the world was still in its perfect state—*before* sin entered it.

The Lord God caused a deep sleep to fall upon Adam, and as he slept, God took a rib from him and fashioned Eve. God then brought Eve to Adam. When Adam saw her he said, "[She is] bone of my bones and flesh of my flesh" (vv. 21–23). In effect he was saying, "I am complete when I am with her."

A High and Holy Title

How does it make you feel to know that you are called to be a helper to your husband? Do you like it? Or do you wish it were different?

We seem to love the idea of God tossing out the stars and calling each of them by name (Psalm 147:4). We are speechless at the very thought of Him, God Almighty, knitting us together in our mothers' wombs and ordaining all our days (Psalm 139:13–16). We are awed when we read that He measured the waters in the hollow of His hand and marked off the heavens by His hand's breadth (Isaiah 40:12). These things only confirm to us what we already know—He is God. Awesome, almighty, and perfect. Yet we tend to balk at our role as helper.

In fact, this role is a reflection of who God is.

A Precious Name

Helper is a title God uses of Himself over and over again in Scripture. The term *helper* is a precious word. There is nothing inferior, demeaning, or second-rate about it.

"So do not fear, for I am with you; do not be dismayed, for I am your God. I will strengthen you and help you" (Isaiah 41:10). In this verse, God is reassuring His people, telling them not to worry or fear because He, the God of the universe, will be their Helper.

A friend told us, "Never once have I thought about being a helper in this way. I thought of it as one of the many things I do. But now I see it as who I am. I no longer see it as *doing* something; I see it as *being* someone. I realize that I've never given it the priority it was meant to have because I was never taught to do so. If Jesus considers being a helper a worthy calling (Hebrews 13:1), then I want to aspire to that calling as well."

Helper is a title God uses of Himself over and over again in Scripture.

This woman had grabbed hold of what being a helper is all about. It's not something you do after you've done everything else. It's not about what you do at all. It's about who you are.

Helper: One who gives assistance or support to another, making life more pleasant or bearable.

Would your husband say that because of you, his life is more pleasant and bearable? Would he say he can depend on you for assistance? For support? Or does he shy away from making even the simplest request, fearing your reaction?

A Stubborn Heart

When I (Connie) first heard this teaching, I thought to myself, *You must be kidding. Are you sure about this? God's will for me in my marriage is to be a helper to my husband? And that's all? Simply a helper. Only a helper?*

The verse had a familiar ring to it, yet there was little doubt in my mind that the words "helper to her husband" weren't meant to stand alone. There must be another phrase qualifying those words. There had to be more to that verse than just that verse!

When I got home, I looked at this verse in other versions of the Bible. They all said the same thing. I was thinking, *Why has no one brought this to my attention before? And why now?*

Little did I realize that I was rapidly approaching the turning point in my marriage.

I was less than excited about the idea at the time, however. If being a helper was what it was all about, I'd far sooner *have* a helper than *be* one. *What a compromise,* I thought, *and what a misuse of the abilities God has given me.* I didn't understand what there was to be excited about. If all the job titles in the world were listed on a sheet of paper and we could choose just one, I frankly didn't think there would be a mad scramble for the title of helper.

In the early years of my marriage, however, I actually had been a devoted helper to my husband. Not because I was focused on God's Word, but because of my deep love for my husband. I delighted in making him happy, and I looked for opportunities to lighten his load. Somewhere along the way, though, I got tired of helping. My enthusiasm faded, and I no longer enjoyed doing this. My delight was no longer found in making him happy, and soon I began to keep score.

Surely, I thought, *it's time for my husband to do his part. I've done my share. Now he can do his.* My plan was quite simple. I would just slip my heart into neutral until my husband caught on.

He didn't catch on very quickly. *This could take longer than I expected*, I said to myself. I dug my heels in a little further, determined to wait him out.

And so began the long journey of waiting for my husband to change. My heart no longer felt like it was in neutral. It was definitely in reverse, and the engine was cold. The young wife who had taken pleasure in tending to her husband's needs was a distant memory. Over time my heart had grown hard. And harder. And harder still.

Things were not working out the way I had envisioned. I shouldn't have been surprised. I was trying to rewrite God's job description to benefit myself. I discovered that neither our hearts nor our wills are able to slip into neutral. They go one way or the other. We are either obeying God, or we are disobeying. At best, using the word *neutral* was an attempt to cloak my disobedience.

When I learned more about God's job description for me as a wife, my heart was stirred. I believe it was the Holy Spirit convicting me of my need to change. It was a humbling time as I considered stepping back into being a wife God's way. I found myself taking small steps, even half steps. I was still uncertain, perhaps because of my lack of knowledge, lack of trust, or not wanting to be the one to change. Probably it was a blend of all three. But my way obviously wasn't working. So I confessed

    my pride,

        my disobedience,

            my contentiousness,

                and my scorekeeping.

I told God that, shaky and unsure as I was, I was willing to do things His way. With a prayer in my heart, I began to reclaim the calling God had given me. I set out, wobbly legs and all, to be a helper to my husband. Once I chose to do that, I began to feel a joy and peace I had not felt for a very long time. I began to experience a deeper relationship with my husband, and with my Lord as well.

How About You?

If you have been resisting God's Word, what is your reason? Could it be pride? Or bitterness? Or an unforgiving spirit toward your husband? In my case (Nancy), it was ignorance.

I feel that I've had two lives in my marriage. For the first twenty-three years I was busy being a wife in whatever manner suited me for the day. I let my emotions rule my behavior. I didn't know God as He reveals Himself in Scripture—I didn't own a Bible until I was forty-one. I certainly had no idea that He had a plan for me as a wife. For more than twenty years, however, after discovering what God's Word has to say about marriage, I have practiced the principles in this book in my marriage, and with His help, I have changed.

THE REASON: MAN'S ALONENESS

It was when the Lord God looked upon the *aloneness* of Adam that He created Eve: "It is not good (sufficient, satisfactory) that the man should be *alone*; I will make him a helper meet (suitable, adapted, complementary) for him" (Genesis 2:18, AMP).

In researching this book, we asked a male friend to ask his Bible study group to fill in a response to this statement: "If there is one thing I miss in my marriage, it is _____." One of the most frequent answers was *companionship*. Men desire companionship with their mates. They long for someone with whom they can share life's experiences. The men's personality traits, income level, and education had nothing to do with their answers. Almost every man in the group listed companionship.

Our friend later told us, "I believe that men are lonelier today than they have ever been. With all the electronics, video games, reading material, sports programs, and endless lists of things you can do to fill up your time, most men have never felt so alone."

Men are lonely today just as Adam was in the Garden of Eden. Because of this aloneness, woman was created. Could it be that man's loneliness today may be in part because women have abandoned their God-given roles and are busy doing their own thing and going their own way? Has this contributed to man's regressing back to the lonely state he knew in the Garden? The question "Would your husband say he feels less alone because you are his wife?" haunted me (Connie). I remember physically cringing as I contemplated this thought. *Maybe it's not as bad as I think,* I told myself. So I asked my husband about it.

He replied, "I've felt alone many times in our marriage. I remember a point when I felt more alone when I was with you than I did when I was by myself. I have never felt more alone than I did at those times."

This was not the reassuring answer I had hoped to hear, yet it came as no surprise. There was a time in our marriage when we both felt that way. There was no talking, no touching, no shared glances, and no laughter.

It is a testimony to God's faithfulness and love that this changed. This occurred when I began to work on my marriage and apply biblical principles. My heart began to soften, and I saw my husband in a completely different light.

Putting Words into Action

What can a woman do to make sure her husband isn't lonely? Simply being there for him is a wonderful way to begin! One way is to show how important he is to you by your attentiveness. How others respond to us shapes the way we see ourselves. Men thrive on positive responses—from their bosses, their coworkers, their customers, but especially from their wives. Is your husband thriving in your home or barely eking out an existence?

My (Connie) grandmother's eyes lit up every time she saw me. She didn't have to utter a single word for me to feel welcome. I could see the sparkle that radiated from those hazel eyes whenever she looked at me. It didn't matter if I was dressed for church or if I'd just come in from making mud pies in her backyard, I felt special every time we were together. She lived on a meager income and left next to nothing financially when she died. But she left me with something that no amount of money can buy—the knowledge that I was of great worth to her.

Do you show your husband that he matters greatly to you? Does he feel special in your presence? It's easy to get caught up in the busyness of life and push him further and further down on your list of priorities. It may seem that he doesn't notice or that he doesn't mind. But he does.

Does your face soften when you look at your husband? Does

your countenance become brighter when he enters the room? Do your eyes convey warmth, or do they send him a message that says he's a long way from where you think he should be as a man, a father, a provider? When he's feeling uncertain or worried, can he look at you and feel encouraged?

What would happen if you began to notice your husband again? If you let him know that you no longer want him to feel alone?

An easy way to get started with this is through something we call "blastoff" and "reentry." It is one of the most effective and powerful things you can do for your husband.

Blastoff

What are mornings like in your home? Just as there are two critical periods in the voyage of a spacecraft—blastoff and reentry—there are also two critical periods in your home each day.

Blastoff is our term for when you and your husband say goodbye to each other in the morning. A dozen other things are probably going on in your home as he (and often you) is trying to get out the door. This is especially true if you have young children.

When your husband is feeling uncertain or worried, can he look at you and feel encouraged?

Mornings are the perfect time to make your husband feel that he is not alone. You may be thinking that there is not time for one more thing in your schedule. Make time! The few minutes you spend sending him off will be one of the best investments you can make in your day—and his.

In chapter 5 we'll go into detail about practical things you can do to control your time, but for now here are a few tips that will help you create more time in the morning and put the "good" back in "good morning."

- Go to bed at a reasonable hour. If you have young children and haven't established a set bedtime for them, do it now. It may be a battle at first, but it is a battle worth fighting, and everyone will benefit once a routine is established.
- Set your snooze alarm to give yourself five to ten minutes of extra wake-up time.
- Get up fifteen to thirty minutes before your household for a quiet time with God. Pray for your husband and your marriage during this time.
- Take some juice or coffee to him as he's waking up or as he's getting ready for work. You'll be surprised at how much this small effort is appreciated.
- Kiss him, hug him, perhaps say something like, "Welcome to your morning," "Good morning," or "I love you." Your attempts may be awkward at first, but you will be amazed at how quickly the awkwardness goes away and a sense of closeness occurs.
- If you can, fix him breakfast. You might set out a pretty tray the night before. Put the dishes, glasses, and silverware on it. In the morning, arrange his cereal, fruit, juice, vitamins, and whatever else he needs. If you have fresh flowers in the yard, include them occasionally. This entire process takes only about three minutes! It's well worth the effort, and it makes many men feel loved and special. You need to adapt these suggestions to fit your circumstances, however. One young bride did this for her new husband. After three weeks, he confided that he wasn't a breakfast man and not a morning talker. So she avoided both, much to his delight.

- If you can do only one thing, when he leaves (or before you do) go to him, look in his eyes, and smile. Give him a loving hug and a kiss. Tell him that you love him and that you hope he has a wonderful day. The tone of your voice should be warm and sincere. It may have been a long time since you've done this, and you may feel awkward at first. Don't worry: Before long it will seem like you've always done it this way.

As a side note, statistics have shown that a successful blastoff is a safeguard against accidents on the way to work.

Reentry

Reentry is the second critical time in your home. This is when you and your husband reunite at the end of the day. The first five minutes you are together set the tone for the rest of the night.

In one installment of the comic strip *Drabble,* Ralph, the husband and father, is pictured coming home from work. He is met at the door by his wife, who says, "Ralph, that faucet you fixed in the upstairs bathroom is still leaking." Then his two younger children greet him with complaints: "Daddy, Patrick's been calling me a fenderhead!" "Have not!" Next, his teenager confesses, "Dad, I parked in a tow-away zone today. Can I borrow $160?" In the last scene, Ralph is staring into his bathroom mirror, talking to his image. "Welcome home, Ralph. Good to see you. How are you doing? Fine. Thanks for asking!"

Is this typical of reentry in your home? Do you look forward to your husband's homecoming each evening, or do you inwardly sigh and think to yourself, *Is he home already?* It is a sad statement if the dog is the only member in his welcoming committee. If your husband gets home before you, find him! Let him know how happy you are to be back with him. Maybe you don't feel happy. You can still greet him with kindness and welcome him home.

Here are some tips to help you with the task of reentry:

- Pray for a warm, loving reunion.
- If you're home first, watch for his return, and if possible walk out to meet him as he gets out of the car. This shows that you actually anticipate his arrival.
- Greet him with warmth and affection. Make it a priority to be the first one to greet him each evening.
- Give him a few minutes to unwind. Men frequently say they need time to "deprogram" after working all day. You may be thinking that you'd like a few minutes to deprogram too because you've worked all day as well, either in or out of the home—or both! Ask the Lord to help you find the time to do that prior to your reunion. It's amazing how refreshing just a few minutes to yourself can be.
- If your husband is a talker, stop what you're doing and talk with him about his day. If he's the nonverbal type, don't press him for details.
- Don't tell him everything that went wrong during the day the minute he steps through the door.
- If your husband enjoys the newspaper when he gets home, don't begrudge his reading it. If he asks whether you've seen a certain article in the newspaper, don't be tempted to tell him that you've been too busy to sit down all day, let alone look at the paper. This kind of self-pity is no fun for him, you, or anyone else within hearing distance.
- Make it your goal each evening to create an atmosphere that you and your husband enjoy.

Successful Launches

Two women we know decided to try this idea of blastoff and reentry. The first woman said:

> I was afraid my husband would fall into a coma if I tried this, so I decided to start slowly. When he left in the morning, I simply said, "Good-bye," which was a big change from totally ignoring his departure. A few days later I added, "I hope you have a good day." Though that sounds simple enough, it had been so long since I had wished him a good day that it was difficult for me. Next, I began walking my husband partway to the door. Then all the way. I began to wave to him from the window as he left. Over time I began to watch for him when he came home. I'd start waving at him when he pulled into the driveway. *One day he waved back!* Before long, I found myself going out to the car to meet him and ask how his day had gone.
>
> To my astonishment, he began to tell me. Not much at first, but over time he told more and more. He has never said anything about the change that has taken place, but I know he notices. Our home is a much happier place.

Said the second woman:

> If you had told me this could make such a difference, I would have laughed out loud. But I was desperate and decided to try. Truthfully, my heart wasn't in it, and I wondered why I should be the one doing the work. I didn't feel that my husband deserved it. He's usually irritable in the mornings because he's tired and irritable in the evenings because he's tired.

Why bother? I thought to myself. I work as well, and I saw this as just one more thing to do before getting out of the house and on my way. Still, I began. Prior to this our paths had rarely crossed in the morning as we both got ready for the day. I think I made him nervous. I was nervous too.

But I continued on. Though change came slowly, when it did occur it brought with it a long-lost feeling of peace and of knowing that what I was doing was right. Over time, this small thing changed both of us. God used my willingness to minister to my husband to soften my heart. My husband noticed, and his heart changed as well. Now it's such a normal part of our day that not doing it would seem strange.

Begin Today

Women have shared with us that blastoff and reentry have been two of the easiest ways to effect change in their homes. What's it like in your home? Are your morning departures for work and arrivals back home smooth? Or are they more the crash-and-burn variety? Is it time for change? *What would happen if the change started with you?* This is a wonderful, nonthreatening way to introduce genuine warmth back into your home. And there's no better time to start than today!

God Helps Us Change

If you're seeing that you've made some poor choices in your marriage, don't feel overwhelmed, discouraged, or alone. Praise God that He is stirring your heart to address some of these things now.

Are you willing to do what you can to show your husband that he is not alone? Would you consider moving into the role God created for you? Your answer may be no right now. *Are you willing to be made willing?* Maybe your prayer should be, "Lord, please help me be willing to be willing."

If you feel God tugging on your heart in this area, set about today to make things right. Whether you've been married for a few months or for decades, it is never too late to begin showing your husband how much he means to you and what a privilege it is to be his wife.

THE RELATIONSHIP: MARRIAGE

The Original Wedding

We have seen that God, not wanting Adam to be alone, fashioned a woman from Adam's rib as he slept:

> So the LORD God caused the man to fall into a deep sleep;
> and while he was sleeping, he took one of the man's ribs
> and closed up the place with flesh. Then the LORD God
> made a woman from the rib he had taken out of the man,
> and he brought her to the man. (Genesis 2:21–22)

How lovely she must have been. She was created in God's own image! We can almost feel God's personal joy as we read the words "He brought her to the man."

When did they first catch sight of each other? Who saw whom first? Could it have been Adam who, awakening from his sleep, heard the rustle of footsteps and noticed the lovely gift God had given him?

The first recorded human words were spoken by Adam: "She shall be called Woman, because she was taken out of Man" (Genesis 2:23, NASB).

Then the Lord God taught the bride and groom His principles for marriage. They were not only for them, but for all generations to come. Now, as then, marriage is to be a commitment of the heart, the will, and the body.

Commitment of the Heart

For this cause a man shall leave his father and his mother..." (Genesis 2:24, NASB)

Have you and your husband done that?

Man is the one that God singles out regarding this issue, but it certainly applies to both of you. This is one of the hardest, but most necessary, things a married couple must do. By "leaving" your mother and father, you put your husband in first place in your heart.

Are you a "daddy's girl"? Do you value your father's opinion more than your husband's? Would you rather spend time with your mother than with your spouse? Your husband can resent this to the point that he no longer seems to care for your parents. Would you choose to give your full allegiance to your husband before any other person?

Don't cling so tightly to your family and their ways that you put a wedge between you and your husband. You are to be working toward unity with your husband and building your own marital relationship and traditions.

Commitment of the Will

"...and shall cleave to his wife." (Genesis 2:24, NASB)

You are to effect a close, loyal, unwavering, permanent relationship with your husband. You are to be faithful to one another until death. This involves choices.

Ed Wheat, in his book *Love Life for Every Married Couple*, describes the choices like this:

> When God planted the garden of our nature and caused the flowering, fruiting love to grow there, He set our will to tend them as a wise gardener. This operation of the will is agape love. Agape love is plugged into an eternal power source and it can go on operating when every other kind of love fails. Not only that, it loves no matter what—no matter how unlovable the other person is.[1]

Some of the things you might consider doing:

- Ridding your mind of the words *separation* and *divorce*
- Refusing thoughts of men from your past
- Refusing to be self-centered
- Never getting in touch with an old flame
- Not telling others about your husband's faults
- Always being faithful (faithfulness is a choice that begins in the mind)
- Upholding your husband's good name
- Not comparing your husband unfavorably with others

Commitment of the Body

And they shall become one flesh. And the man and his wife were both naked and were not ashamed. (Genesis 2:24–25, NASB)

Isn't this a wonderfully explicit sexual picture? Sex is God's wedding gift. He created you to relish this aspect of marriage.

God's speaking about sex to Adam and Eve was the first thing they heard together as a couple. He intended for them to love each other. One precious expression of their love would be delighting in each other physically. Perhaps that is why Eve's wedding dress was simply her body.

To deny the physical aspect of your marriage is to diminish one of God's greatest gifts to you and your husband. To withhold yourself from your husband, except by mutual agreement, is destructive and wrong (1 Corinthians 7:4–5, NASB). A lack of physical closeness can greatly affect emotional and spiritual closeness. There is something mysteriously wonderful about the physicalness of marriage and touching.

When I (Nancy) lie down in bed each night with my husband, it is with deep elation and thanksgiving for him. I often tell him that this is the most wonderful moment of my day—to experience his nearness. Many couples that have been married as long as we have sleep in separate rooms. This seems sad to me. There is something special about sleeping side by side, touching. In the coldness of this world, the warmest place you know should be your marriage bed.

RECONSIDERING YOUR ROLE

We have examined the wife's role, the reason for this role, and the context in which this God-given role can be fulfilled. Are you willing to reconsider your role in your marriage? Are you willing to pick up the role of wife, God's way? Are you committed to carrying out this role, regardless of what your husband's response is?

There are no limits to what God can do through a heart that is yielded to Him in obedience and trust. In the following chapters, we will review why we struggle with our helper role, examine two foundational principles that will empower us to fulfill God's will for us as wives, and look at some suggestions about how we can deal practically with this wonderful calling.

God said, "It is not good for the man to be alone. I will make a helper suitable for him."

We are called to be that helper.

What a challenge…

What a privilege…

What a Creator!

Chapter Two: Choices! Choices! Choices!

Choices! Choices! Choices! We start making them as soon as our eyes open in the morning. Should I sleep ten more minutes or get up? What's for breakfast? What should I wear? What will I do today?

Some are inconsequential, but some have consequences that can forever alter your world—because some choices are really veiled temptations. The mother of mankind, Eve, faced one temptation that quickly tripled. She saw that the tree was good for food—the lust of the flesh. That it was pleasing to the eyes—the lust of the eyes. And that it would make one wise—the pride of life. She chose the forbidden fruit (Genesis 3; 1 John 2:16).

Jesus was tempted in the same three ways. Yet He overcame temptation, saying: "It is written…it is written…it is written…. And the devil left Him" (Matthew 4:3–4; 6–7; 10–11).

Arm yourself and resist temptation. In doing so, you will be blessed!

Choices! Choices! Choices!

You are always free to choose your actions,
but never free to choose your consequences.

I (Nancy) thought we had just become rich. We were moving to Denver, and my husband's salary had doubled. Within a few months, I had a beautiful home built to my specifications, furniture that coordinated perfectly, and a new sports car. This was near the end of the seventies. The "me generation" was just beginning, and I was at the front of the line.

However, due to my reckless spending, we were soon in a financial crunch. I wondered how I could have done this to my husband and children. All my husband said to me was, "You're going to have to get a job and help pay down this debt." So I did.

I still remember one of our daughters calling me at work one day. She had just arrived home from school, and it was her birthday. "I'm going to make my birthday cake now," she told me. Had I not gotten us into that situation, I would have been able to welcome my daughter home with a hug, her birthday cake already baked. I may have called Denver home, but the state I lived in was depression, and the suburb was guilt.

Like Eve, I had been duped into thinking that this "one little thing" could make me happy. In my case, it was an upscale lifestyle and all that went with it. I somehow thought that these worldly goods would elevate me to a whole new level of life.

But I was wrong. I had been deceived. Satan had gotten me to focus my attention on myself. It was a hard lesson to learn regarding expensive tastes, but God used the pit I had dug to begin my journey to knowing Him as Savior and Lord.

Two years later I bought my first Bible. Two years after that I became involved in a Bible study and learned that Jesus had paid for all my sins on the cross. And the following year I learned that, like all of us, I was born a daughter of Eve.

What does this have to do with our role as wives in marriage today? Understanding what went on in the Garden helps us pinpoint why women resist their own role as well as their husbands' in marriage. We believe that women crave rulership in marriage. This is a consequence of Eve's choice. Because of Adam and Eve's disobedience, God amended the male and female roles. Eve would thereafter be "ruled" by Adam, which is a far more serious state than being "led" by his loving authority.

Let's take another look at what happened in the Garden in order to see how we can begin to reclaim our high calling as wives and get around the roadblocks in our marriages.

FRUIT CAN BE SO APPEALING

The LORD God commanded the man, saying, "From any tree of the garden you may eat freely; but from the tree of the knowledge of good and evil you shall not eat, for in the day that you eat from it you shall surely die." (Genesis 2:16–17, NASB)

Eve was the first person ever to struggle with temptation. The handprint of God must have been fresh upon her when that sly serpent entered her world. This creature was craftier than all of the other animals. The choice that would devastate her life was to eat from a piece of fruit that hung from a forbidden tree. That same serpent tempts us today with worldly enticements that run counter to the Word of God.

DID GOD REALLY SAY...?

God had given Eve dominion over this very serpent when He authorized her and Adam to rule over every living thing. She could have banished him from her sight, but instead she was open and approachable and allowed him to engage her in conversation. He had an offer, and she was interested. With shrewd deliberation, he questioned her understanding of what God had said:

> He said to the woman, "Did God really say, 'You must not eat from any tree in the Garden'?" (Genesis 3:1)

What he was really asking was this: "Are you sure, Eve? Are you 100 percent sure? How could this be? It makes no sense. Let me clarify this for you."

Do you notice that when Satan questioned Eve, he made his question sound very similar to what God had actually said? God said they could eat from any tree *except one*. Satan asked whether they could eat from *any tree at all.* He was creating confusion regarding God's Word, making Eve think that what God said was not what He really meant. *The difference between God's Word and Satan's version of it is the difference between the truth and a lie.*

Caught off guard, Eve found herself considering the serpent's words. Perhaps she was vulnerable because she had not heard the words from God firsthand. She hadn't yet been created when God spoke them to Adam. Obviously, though, Adam had told her what God said, and now the serpent was asking her to consider his view.

Eve responded to him, "We may eat fruit from the trees in the garden, but God did say, 'You must not eat fruit from the tree that is in the middle of the garden, and you must not touch it, or you will die'" (Genesis 3:2–3).

Eve had already added her own twist to what God said. He didn't mention touching the tree; He said only that they were not to eat from it.

The serpent still tries to rework God's Word in our lives. His version is usually easy on our ears. He says what we think we want to hear.

Has Satan engaged you in conversation recently? Have you added your own twist to God's Word? Has he caused you to doubt God? Doubt is an insidious thing. It creeps into your life so slowly and so quietly that you may not even realize it's there.

When I was growing up, my (Connie) family lived in a house with a small bathroom at the back. Every now and then my oldest sister would get upset with me over something and would chase me. I would run through the house and into the bathroom. Once there, I would hurriedly try to slam the door shut, locking it as I closed it. Most of the time I was successful, but occasionally she would get there in time to get just the toe of her shoe between the door and the frame. I knew it would be mere moments before she'd wedge her arm through the door, and then her shoulder, and then her whole body. She was always delighted when this happened, but I was not.

Satan needs only a crack for doubt to come oozing into your life, and he's delighted when you begin to consider forbidden fruit. These might be thoughts of another man or that life would be so much easier if only your husband weren't a part of it. The fruit represents many different things in your life, but at its core, it stands for the temptation to disobey God's Word.

DISTORTING GOD'S WORD

After getting Eve's attention and questioning her, the serpent took the simplicity of God's Word and contradicted it, telling her that she would not surely die as God had said. In fact, he assured her that when she ate from the fruit, her eyes would be opened and she would be like God, knowing good and evil.

With bold, contemptible brazenness the serpent offered to correct God's Word. What an absurd thought, but he stopped at nothing to convince Eve to disobey. He was unrelenting in his pursuit of Eve, *just as he is with us today.*

The serpent still tries to rework God's Word in our lives. His version is usually easy on our ears. He says what we think we want to hear. He may even weave in just enough truth to make us think that what we're doing actually has some spiritual merit, but of course it doesn't!

The Lie

The serpent busily wove a web of lies and deceit around Eve. He talked and she listened. The longer she listened, the more confused she became. Bit by bit he lured her. Into his plan. Away from God's plan.

He was saying: "You *can* eat from that tree, Eve. There's no reason to deprive yourself any longer. You won't die! He knows very well that the instant you eat from it you will be like Him—able to distinguish good from evil." Satan tempted Eve with the very thing that caused his own fall—the desire to be like God (Ezekiel 28:2, 12–17).

Eve's Choice

Eve pondered the serpent's words. Was she convinced when the serpent assured her that she could actually be like God? This must have been an amazing thought. Surely the serpent had her full attention now. Who wouldn't want to be like Him? Who wouldn't eat from the tree if that was the end result?

Her brow furrowed as she thought the matter over. Had she heard correctly? Had Adam? Maybe he had forgotten to pass this part on to her. Did God really mean what He had said?

Eve considered the serpent's words. His interpretation seemed so logical. He spoke so boldly. So confidently. So persuasively. The longer she thought, the more she weakened. Eve made her choice. Did all of creation weep when she sank her teeth into the forbidden fruit?

Eve's fall into sin was a progressive one.

First: She listened to the serpent's words.

Second: She dialogued with him.

Third: She considered his lies.

Fourth: She chose to believe them.

Fifth: She disobeyed God.

How can you protect yourself against the enemy? One of the best ways is to know what the Word of God says. Then, when confronted with temptation, you are armed. The Bible calls God's Word the sword of the Spirit (Ephesians 6:17).

When treasury agents are trained to recognize counterfeit money, they study the real thing. They become so well acquainted with true currency that they can quickly spot the false. So it should be with us. We should be so familiar with God's Word that we immediately recognize an altered version of it.

Before she acted, Eve should have gone to God for clarification of what He had said, but she didn't. Instead, she permitted Satan to lead her, step by slippery step, into the quagmire of disobedience.

How do you feel about God's directives for your life? It's not unusual for worldly women today to laugh at them. Tragically, Christian women do this as well. We don't realize that the same crafty serpent who lured Eve is now luring us. The ploy he uses is dissatisfaction with our roles in marriage, yet we often remain oblivious or apathetic. Could it be that we have gone our own way for so long that we no longer recognize our behavior as sinful, but instead see it as normal?

We have been barraged from every angle with the message that the Bible is no longer applicable for today. Talk shows use biblical truths as fodder for audience ridicule. Radio programs tell us to do whatever it takes, with whomever it takes, to find our happiness for the moment. Tragically, our children take in this information and learn the same patterns for their own lives.

THEN AND NOW

It was a disastrous thing when Eve stopped believing God's Word and bought into the serpent's false promises. With that single bite, Eve introduced disobedience into a perfect world. Her life was about to change dramatically. Her actions would affect every living being from that day forward. Because of this sin, we are still susceptible to Satan's lies today.

Over and over again he whispers persuasively, *"Did God really say…?"*

Did God really say…you are called to be a helper to your husband? What an old-fashioned, outdated plan.

Did God really say…your husband is to be the leader in your home when you are so much more gifted?

Did God really say…you should be a godly wife? Your husband is so far from being a godly husband. What's right or fair about that?

STANDING BEFORE GOD

After Eve ate from the tree, she passed the fruit to Adam, and he too ate from it. Afterward in their shame, they tried to hide from God. When He found them, God asked, "Have you eaten from the tree that I commanded you not to eat from?" (Genesis 3:11).

What utter shame and horror they must have felt. They had came face-to-face with temptation and given in, and now they stood face-to-face with God. They both knew they had disobeyed His command. It must have been sheer agony to stand before almighty God, knowing they had chosen their way over His.

Most of us look at Eve and wonder how she could have possibly disobeyed God. The right choice seems so obvious to us. Yet every day we make choices, as Eve did, and too often we choose her way. Generally it's easier to pinpoint sin in another's life than in our own.

We are daughters of Eve, and because of that, we sin. Her sin in the Garden is no greater than the sins we commit every day, yet we tend to dilute our disobedience and justify our actions. Our attitude toward sin has become casual. A missionary friend put it like this: "We've forgotten how God *hates* sin—how He *despises* it. We've become far too comfortable with it, forgetting that it goes against the very character of God. As a result, we allow it greater and greater entrance into our lives, sometimes without as much as a second glance."

Frequently when we do stop and consider sin in our lives, we have a tendency to point the finger at someone else, as Adam and Eve did.

THE CHAIN OF BLAMING OTHERS

God's question to Adam and Eve was quite simple: Had they eaten from the tree or not? Their answers, however, were far from simple. They did some artful dodging. We are about to see the first documented case of something we are all too familiar with: blaming others for our own sin.

Being a quick thinker, but apparently struggling with memory loss, Adam said, "The woman *you* put here with me—she gave me some fruit from the tree, and I ate it" (Genesis 3:12). He blamed not only Eve but also God for giving him the woman in the first place. The Lord turned to Eve, and she responded, "The *serpent* deceived me, and I ate" (Genesis 3:13). And so began the chain of blaming others for our own sin. It continues today.

Do you ever fall into that trap? Whom or what do you blame when you disobey God?

- Your husband
- Your kids
- Your upbringing
- Your schedule
- Your finances
- Stress
- Headaches
- Heartaches

The only person to blame when you choose to disobey is yourself. Jesus says, "If anyone loves me, he will obey my teaching.… He who does not love me will not obey my teaching" (John 14:23–24). Do you love Jesus? Do you obey His Word? According to this verse, you can't say yes to one and no to the other because your love or lack of love is demonstrated by your obedience.

A WOMAN'S INFLUENCE

The fact that a woman has tremendous influence in a man's life was dramatically proven when Eve passed the fruit to Adam and he ate from it. God had spoken *directly* to him and told him not to eat from it. Yet in the presence of Eve, his resolve softened, and he chose to disobey God. It is impossible to overstate the incredible influence Eve had in his life.

We cannot take this principle lightly in our own lives today. We greatly influence our husbands' lives and choices. A woman's ability to get her husband to do what she wants has not weakened since the Garden. She can even do this in the name of godliness. This is so powerful that she must constantly check herself to see that she isn't misusing this power.

Do you misuse the influence you have in your husband's life? Do you offer anything to him that is not pleasing to God? Eve did, and because of this she, along with Adam, faced severe consequences.

CONSEQUENCES

Sin never visits us alone. It travels with a companion called *consequence*. Every time you sin, there is a consequence. This was seen first in the Garden immediately after Adam and Eve chose to disobey God.

God prefaced Adam's consequences with the words "Because you listened to your wife" (Genesis 3:17). Adam's consequences were a direct result of Eve's influence. Even though Adam had free will and was responsible for his disobedience, Eve's part in this did not go unnoticed. God sees what we do in our husbands' lives! What a motivation this should be to us as wives.

God went on to tell Adam that from then on his labor would be exhausting because of a curse on the ground. Adam had worked before the Fall, but now his work would be toilsome.

Eve's Role Is Amended by God

Eve's consequences would include greater pain in childbearing, and we're told that her desire and craving would be for her husband:

"Yet your desire *and* craving will be for your husband, and he will rule over you" (Genesis 3:16, AMP).

Certainly the meaning here is deeper than that a woman would continue to desire her husband sexually. *Crave* means to demand, to want mastery over, to want greatly, to need as one needs drugs. There is nothing passive about craving.

What is it that women crave today perhaps more than anything else? Could it be that what we crave refers to the second part of woman's consequence for her sin? *Is it the desire to rule over our husbands?*

Susan Foh, in her book *Women and the Word of God: A Response to Biblical Feminism,* explains:

> The "curse" here describes the beginning of the battle of the sexes. After the fall, the husband no longer rules easily; he must fight for his headship. The woman's desire is to control her husband (to usurp his divinely appointed headship), and he must master her, if he can. Sin has corrupted both the willing submission of the wife and the loving headship of the husband. And so, the rule of love founded in paradise is replaced by struggle, tyranny, domination, and manipulation.[1]

Never should Adam have followed Eve's lead. She desired to take the lead from her husband and have him do what she wanted. Now both were condemned. Her punishment matched her sin: Man was to rule over her, not simply lead her. And man was punished for submitting to her lead. It's important to remember that this is not a passage about husband and wife relationships, as we find in later revelation in the New Testament. This is a passage about consequences—the punishment of mankind for sin.

Before the Fall, there was a positive complementary relationship in which the husband was the leader and the woman his complement. But since the Fall, man *rules*. Throughout history women have been ruled over by men, often cruelly. The New Testament teaches the husband how to rule in this fallen world with *love* for his wife, rather than through tyranny. He is told to love his wife in order to temper the judgment of rulership over the woman so it is done in the way that was proper before the Fall.

In the New Testament the woman is asked to respect her husband's leadership, the very thing she was trying to supplant when she sinned, which then prompted the man to sin.

It appears to us that the New Testament is trying to get man and wife back into a more complementary relationship, similar to what existed before the Fall while recognizing the consequences of the Fall.

Undoubtedly, Eve felt hopeless and lost as she realized just how much that bite of fruit had cost. Surely she clung to the words God had spoken to the serpent:

> "I will put enmity between you and the woman, and between
> your seed and her seed; he shall bruise you on the head, and
> you shall bruise him on the heel." (Genesis 3:15, NASB)

From that point forward, there would be a continuous struggle between opposing forces: Satan and man. Yet the seed of woman would deliver the fatal blow to Satan. You and I know who that is—Jesus! He is the holy offspring of Mary, who conceived Him as the Holy Spirit came upon her.

In His mercy and love, God forced Adam and Eve out of the Garden, blocking their approach to the tree of life. If they had continued to eat of that tree, they would have stayed perpetually locked in their sin.

Praise God, you and I live on this side of the Cross! Jesus became the curse for us so that we could have eternal life. He came to earth to die on the cross to pay the price for our sins.

Living on this side of the Cross simply means that through the blood of Jesus, those who have asked Him to be their Savior have the power to live their lives in a new way, based on the truth of God's Word.

Have you taken that step and accepted Jesus as your Savior? We've outlined the simple steps of how to do so.

THE PLAN OF SALVATION

To receive Christ you need to do four things:

1. ADMIT your spiritual need: "I am a sinner."
2. REPENT and be willing to turn from your sin.
3. BELIEVE that Jesus Christ died for you on the cross.
4. RECEIVE, through prayer, Jesus Christ into your heart and life.[2]

This plan is seen in Scripture in the following verses: John 1:12; 3:16; Romans 3:23; 1 John 1:7–10.

Romans 10:13 says, "Everyone who calls on the name of the Lord will be saved." What might you pray if you wish to do this? Perhaps a prayer like this:

Dear Jesus,

I admit that I am a sinner. I want to turn from my sins. I believe that You died on the cross for me. I ask You to come into

*my heart and my life as my Lord and Savior. Thank You for
dying on the cross for me and for saving me. Amen.*

Once you do this, you are born again into the family of God.
This is all that is required to enter the kingdom of God (John 3:7).

My (Connie) friends and I used to discuss what being "born
again" meant. It wasn't a commonly used term when I was young.
I wasn't sure what it meant and even less sure that I needed it.
Although I had accepted Christ at an early age, I worried for years
that I hadn't done enough to assure that I would go to heaven and
be with Him when I died. It was not until adulthood that I learned
I had done all that was needed. And if you have prayed to trust
Christ as your Savior, you have too. Certainly your spiritual growth
will always be in process, but you are assured salvation the instant
you receive Christ.

Jesus wants to be your Savior. No matter where you've been, what
you've done, or what kind of life you're currently leading, He longs
for you to ask Him into your heart. His death on the cross covered
everything. *All you've done or could do, except reject Him, is covered by
His blood.*

Not long ago, very early in the morning, I (Connie) pulled into
the parking lot of the hospital where my husband works. It was not
yet five o'clock, and the front doors were still locked. As I got out
of my car, I noticed a young couple standing at the revolving doors,
trying to force them open. The husband was pushing with all his
might, but they wouldn't budge. As I got closer, the woman turned
toward her husband with a look of desperation on her face. She was
near tears. As she turned, I saw that she was nine months pregnant,
dressed in her robe, and in hard labor. "The doors are locked and
we can't get in," the man cried out to me as I approached. "My wife's

in labor. We've got to get inside." He was very young, and his voice cracked with urgency and fear.

I was familiar with the hospital and knew that a side door just a few steps away was most likely open. And if it wasn't, there was a phone tucked inside a box nearby, and we could call the security office. With a click of a button, they could unlock the doors. We tried the side door and it opened. The couple was so relieved. I ran to the elevator and pressed the button for the ob-gyn floor, holding the doors open for them. "Is this your first?" I asked.

"Yes," the young man said, "and we think it's a boy!"

I wished them well, and they were gone.

Somewhere out there is a little child whose parents will one day tell him that when they finally got Mom to the hospital, the doors were locked and they didn't know how to get inside until someone showed them.

The door of heaven is open to you today. Jesus Himself unlocked the door for those who would receive Him by faith. There is no reason to stand outside anymore. The only thing needed for admission is for you to repent of your sins and trust Jesus as your Savior. If you haven't done this, won't you consider doing so now?

If you've just made this decision, or if you are a new Christian, seek out a Bible-teaching church in your area. Ask God to help you find someone who will help you grow in your spiritual walk.

INTERACTION BASED ON LOVE

Jesus showed us by His life how to live and how to love. No longer do we have to live under the curse; we have the ability to live with freedom (Galatians 5). The power struggle for leadership in the home can be a thing of the past.

There is a new God-given way to be a husband and wife. Our interaction with each other is to be based on love (Ephesians 5:1–2). A husband is to love his wife as Christ loved the church; a wife is to respect and submit to her husband as to the Lord (vv. 22, 25). These principles will be discussed more fully in chapter 5.

Because of Jesus, we have available to us a new life, a new nature, and a new freedom. Sin's power over us is broken. We are no longer under its control. We share in Jesus' life. We can consider ourselves to be dead to sin, but alive to God. We have been freed from sin. The penalty for sin and its power over our lives died with Jesus on the cross.

Even though we still feel like sinning, and sometimes do, we are no longer slaves to our sinful nature. Now we can choose to live for Christ.

TIMELESS QUESTIONS

Did you know that the first two questions in the Bible occurred when Adam and Eve ate of the fruit?

The first question, "Did God really say, 'You must not eat from any tree in the garden'?" (Genesis 3:1), was asked by the serpent. This question was the door by which sin entered the world. Satan's motive in asking this of Eve was to cause her to disobey God. His motive today is unchanged.

The second question, "Where are you?" (Genesis 3:9), was asked by God. As He walked through the Garden in the cool of the day, He asked Adam where he was, knowing full well that he and Eve were hiding because of their sin.

Perhaps you could apply this same question in your marriage: *Where are you?* Are you following God's plan for your marriage? Are you bringing honor to God in your role as a wife, or would you too be tempted to hide from God?

Don't allow yourself to be taunted by the enemy's words: *Did He really say…?* Don't allow Satan's lies to win the battle regarding your actions. Don't permit him to convince you that your husband doesn't deserve a godly wife. *It is the Lord Himself who desires your godliness and obedience.*

Throughout the book, we will give you many ideas about being a helper to your husband in obedience to your calling as a wife. In the next two chapters, we'll examine two areas that are foundational to becoming empowered to be a godly wife. However, just as we have seen in the life of Eve and in our own lives, this involves choices. One of the ways we can learn to persist in our efforts to become godly wives is to learn to choose right actions over our feelings.

ACTION VERSUS FEELING

By and large, most women operate on their feelings. But these very feelings often get us off track. If we're upset or irritated with our husbands, it shows in our actions toward them. Or if we think we're doing our part but feel that they're not doing theirs, we shut down. We want to be godly wives—as long as our husbands are treating us as we think they should. Our actions toward our husbands are often determined by whether we feel they deserve such treatment. The minute they step over a certain line, which has been predetermined by us, our efforts stop.

What would happen in a marriage if, through the Holy Spirit's power, a woman chose to act in godly ways regardless of her feelings?

In their book *Happiness Is a Choice,* Frank B. Minirth and Paul

D. Meier say that it's fine to try to understand our feelings as best we can, but the real focus should not be on our feelings but on our behavior. "You don't do what you do because you feel the way you feel—you feel the way you feel because you do what you do." They go on to explain, "Think about that for a moment. In other words, your actions (godly or ungodly) will determine how you feel. If you choose to love your mate, for example, and choose to act lovingly and respectfully toward your mate, the feelings of love will follow whether it was there before or not."[3]

"You don't do what you do because you feel the way you feel—you feel the way you feel because you do what you do."

Feelings are natural and normal, but we have little control over them. What we do have control over is our behavior. If we desire to be godly wives, we must carefully and prayerfully choose what our actions will be and let them take priority over what we happen to be feeling at the moment.

WHO'S DRIVING YOUR CAR?

To paint a clearer picture, think of your feelings and actions as if they were passengers in an automobile. Who is behind the wheel, steering your car? If you're like most women, your *feelings* are doing the driving and your *actions* are in the backseat.

The only thing necessary for your actions to be doing the driving is for you to put them behind the steering wheel. To do this, you will need to remove your feelings from the driver's seat and put them in the backseat.

At first your car may careen wildly back and forth across the road—it may have been a while since your actions have done any steering. But don't give up! Your actions may be hesitant to drive the car and your feelings will be trying to grab the wheel because they don't like sitting in the backseat, but don't give up! Keep your feelings in the backseat, and train your actions to drive.

As you weather the bumps and curves you'll encounter, the trip will begin to smooth out, and over time your actions will drive the car with ease and expertise.

Remember one thing though: No matter how loudly your feelings scream from the backseat, leave them there. As you allow your actions to navigate your car, your feelings will begin to follow. Maybe not immediately and maybe not naturally at first, but eventually they will fall into line with your actions.

When I (Connie) heard this teaching, I thought to myself, *How can I possibly act in a way I do not feel?* It sounded impossible, unpleasant, and hypocritical. The thing that bothered me the most, however, was that I didn't think my husband deserved such treatment. But I was tired of

living in frustration…

making all the rules…

changing all the rules…

being the judge and jury…

having a heart of stone…

being a poor model to my children…

My marital roller coaster seemed to take more and more energy to get to the top of the track. In fact, it had been a very long time since we had been anywhere near the top. What did I have to lose? I humbly asked God to help me:

…Give up my pride

…Stop keeping score

…Soften my stony heart

…Let go of my bitterness

…Put my husband before myself

…Put my husband before my children

…Stop thinking that I always knew best

…Rekindle the love and joy that I once felt

I asked Him to help me start acting the way I wanted to feel and stop being controlled by the feelings that raged within me. With His help, I wrenched my feelings out of the driver's seat and put them in the backseat. Then I cleaned the rust off my rarely used actions and nervously put them behind the wheel of my car. I took a deep breath and stepped out of my comfort zone a little bit. And then a little more. And even more. The car lurched and jerked and sputtered and spewed, but it kept going.

As I write this, tears come to my eyes as I remember how God was there for me—how He held my hand as I shakily drove down this unknown path. How He assured me that this was right when my pride tried to tell me otherwise. And how He encouraged and blessed me as I began to say and do things for my husband that I hadn't said or done in a very long time.

I can't begin to tell you the joy I felt as my heart began to soften. And as it softened, my husband began responding. I no longer had him backed into a corner, daring him to come out. He no longer felt like he was dodging mines in a minefield, never quite knowing when one would erupt. I had finally given him some freedom to be who he was without instant retaliation when he wasn't who I wanted him to be.

My feelings were beginning to catch up with my actions. And no one was more surprised than I was. My only regret was that I hadn't chosen to do this sooner.

If you've never chosen actions like this before, will your husband think things are suddenly strange? Will he even notice? Most likely he will. He may even question why you're acting in such a way. But you know why! And God knows you're doing it out of a desire to be a godly wife, knowing it brings honor and glory to Jesus Christ.

What better reason is there to begin?

Part Two

THE . .
Necessities

Chapter Three: Let Freedom Ring

A fragrance exists today that is far more beautiful than anything you can buy at the cosmetics counter of the nicest store. It is priceless, yet it is freely available to all who desire it: rich, poor, educated, illiterate—to all ages, races, incomes, and professions. It is available to kings and queens, to common thieves, to you and me.

The fragrance is forgiveness—a fragrance so powerful it can transform your life. A fragrance so beautiful it can soften bitter hearts. A fragrance so sweet it will cause others to look at you and wonder just what it is that makes you so different.

Forgiveness—something that was freely given on the cross and something we can freely give others. It is life changing, God honoring, and the key to successful relationships.

Forgiveness—have you accepted His priceless gift?

Let Freedom Ring

*Forgiveness is the fragrance of the violet
on the heel that crushed it.*

MARK TWAIN

A friend of ours recently told us about her and her husband sitting at the dinner table one night and talking about the important events that marked their twenty years of marriage. They spoke of their wedding, their first home, a completed education, dozens of friends, several moves, and finally, the births of their children.

As they thought back over those times, her husband said that something else stood out in his mind, perhaps eclipsing everything that they had just discussed. Our friend had no idea what it was. Her husband was not one for details and remembered little of past events.

"I remember the evening as if it happened yesterday," he said. "It was the night you told me you no longer held against me the unhappy years in our marriage. You said you forgave me and suggested we bury those sad times and set about building new memories to replace them. I knew that I had been hard on you in the past and that the rift between us was due largely to that. I knew also that

I had never really taken full ownership of the hurt and rejection that resulted, preferring instead to let bygones be bygones. So when you said those words to me, it was as if a huge weight was lifted from my shoulders. I felt free. I felt hopeful. I felt forgiven. I felt alive again, in a way I had not felt for a very long time."

Our friend was flabbergasted. She had no idea her words had so profoundly affected him. As he told her later, he felt that the course of their marriage was redirected that evening; no longer would the veil of unforgivingness constantly cloud their marriage.

As she reflected she realized how, almost nonchalantly, she had allowed him to live with the pain and guilt of knowing he had hurt her. In fact, some days she even encouraged it. Yes, he had been hard on her in their early years, but surely she had retaliated by being hard on him in a far worse way.

"What prompted your seemingly sudden forgiveness?" we asked her.

"I was at a point in my life where I desired an intimate relationship with God—I had kept Him at arm's length for so long. I knew, however, that for this to happen, I would have to deal with my lack of forgiveness. I believe this was the primary hindrance to my having an intimate relationship with God. That was the motivating factor," she said.

"Naively, I thought I was doing my husband a favor by wiping the slate clean. However, I discovered that *I* was the one who benefited most. No longer did the pall of unforgivingness permeate my heart and home. Our marriage gears began moving forward again. They had been motionless for so long, locked tightly around old hurts from the past. I thought they had come to a grinding halt because of my husband. Looking back, however, I see that it was my lack of forgiveness that prevented our forward growth. When I forgave my husband, we felt as though we were starting over, and in a sense we were. Our marriage was changed, and I was changed, the day I chose forgiveness."

Are your marriage gears as tightly locked as this woman's were? There is nothing like the oil of forgiveness to get them moving again! It is impossible to overstate the importance of forgiveness in your role as wife. We feel this is one of the most misunderstood, least practiced principles in Scripture. A lack of forgiveness puts roadblocks in your marriage and short-circuits your ability to be a helper to your husband. As you will discover in the pages ahead, forgiveness changes lives and allows you to have a full, vibrant relationship with God.

THE POWER OF FORGIVENESS

This subject of forgiveness is dear to both of us because we were both unforgivers. We were quick to anger and slow to forgive. We never analyzed it; we just thought, *That's the way feelings work.* We would wait until we no longer felt angry to forgive our husbands for whatever we were holding against them. Our feelings dictated our choices. Because of a lack of understanding in this area, we were held hostage by our unforgivingness, even erroneously thinking at times that we had no choice in the matter. We discovered how ridiculous it is to live this way.

Let me (Nancy) give you an example. Ray and I had been married for six years. We had four children, a small house, and furniture that had seen better days. The only really nice thing I owned was a set of bright red canisters my sister had given me. Every time

I saw them I felt special. One day Ray was on the phone and extended the long cord attached to the kitchen wall to its limit, probably to fetch a child. As he did, he inadvertently caught the lid of one of the canisters, causing it to fall to the floor and break. I was inconsolable. Ray was very sorry and asked me to forgive him. But I couldn't. Isn't that absurd? So I wallowed in my sorrow and distanced myself from him. Of course, this quickly spilled over into our communication—I was chilly, if I even spoke.

I was a hostage to my feelings. I had no idea at the time that I could free myself and my marriage from this situation. It was years before I broke out of this fruitless way of living.

Understanding and applying the magnificent antidote of quick forgiveness is the privilege of a real helper in a marriage. In fact, it is essential to any successful relationship, not just one between a husband and wife. Incidentally, by God's grace, He has given both of our husbands a "supernatural amnesia" about our early years as unforgiving wives.

Learning to forgive our husbands freed us from the shackles of allowing our emotions to take precedence in our marriages. Although it was difficult at first, we knew we were pleasing God, which is what kept us going forward when we felt unforgiving. To our surprise, it became easier and easier, although we had (and still have) our days.

Jesus addressed the importance of forgiveness when He instructed the disciples how to pray. After finishing what we know as the Lord's Prayer, He said, "For if you forgive men when they sin against you, your heavenly Father will also forgive you. But if you do not forgive men their sins, your Father will not forgive your sins" (Matthew 6:14–15).

Did you notice that the only point in the Lord's Prayer Jesus emphasized was about forgiveness? Certainly if He is instructing us how to pray, every word is of utmost significance. But it's interesting to note that He addressed forgiveness an additional time.

Next to your salvation, forgiveness may be the most important issue you face in your lifetime. As you apply some of the following principles to your life, you will see why you are the way you are and why you keep doing the things you do. You may also gain insight into why your husband, children, parents, or friends behave the way they do. You will learn why your relationships with your husband and others may be so erratic—warm and loving one minute, cold as ice the next.

Are your feelings holding you captive? Are you exhausted from waiting for "just the right time" to forgive your spouse for whatever it is you're angry about? Don't wait! Life is far too short and your relationships much too important to wait a moment longer.

Understanding the principles of forgiveness will transform your life and the lives of those close to you. The motive for forgiving is simple: Jesus requires it. If we want to be like Him, then we must choose to forgive. Let's look at the basic principles.

PRINCIPLE 1: FORGIVENESS IS ACCOMPLISHED THROUGH CHRIST'S POWER

The power to forgive comes through Christ. His death on the cross enables us to forgive. Through that act, forgiveness spills out onto everyone who receives Him as Savior. You, in turn, are able to extend this same forgiveness to others.

Not long ago we heard the story of a woman who had experienced severe pain and abuse when she was growing up. As an adult, many years later, she accepted Christ as her Savior. Through tears, she told us how she then was able to forgive those who had hurt her. Previously, although she had tried, she had no power to do this because the source of forgiveness wasn't living in her.

Knowing Christ as your Savior is only the beginning to unlocking the doors of forgiveness. Many people can know Him as Savior, yet continue to live their lives locked in the grip of unforgivingness. Such was the case with Carol.

A Daughter's Heartache

Carol appears to have it all. In her thirties, she is tall, slender, attractive, and energetic. She has a handsome and adoring husband, two well-adjusted teenagers, a beautiful home, a great job, extended family support, and is actively involved in her community. More important, she has known the Lord for years.

Few people would guess that Carol struggles with something that causes her great grief and sadness. Over the years it has filled her with a negative, critical spirit that she masterfully covers up whenever she is in public. Outward appearances show a woman who is happy, yet if you knew Carol well, she would tell you that her heart aches almost every day. She longs for true joy and contentment, but thus far they have eluded her. The problem? Carol is an unforgiver. She was raised in a loving, Christian home, but her parents always favored her brother. Because of this, Carol harbors deep resentment. Both her brother and parents live nearby, so she is faced constantly with the situation.

"I've tried to forgive my parents, but can't seem to. Just when I think I have, something else happens, and I'm right back where I was. They make such an effort to be part of my brother's life. They drive right past my house on their way to visit him, yet rarely stop to see me.

"It was bad enough before he had children because until then they treated all of their grandchildren the same way. Now my brother's children are favored openly. They catered to my brother all of his life and now cater to his children. Their favoritism has extended to another generation. My children notice it—how could they not? It's one thing when they slight me, but it's an entirely different matter when they slight my children."

People close to the family would agree that partiality is shown. One of Carol's siblings overheard two aunts discussing the situation. "They are proud of all their kids," they said, speaking of her parents, "but Mike is their pride *and* joy."

Carol holds unforgivingness in her heart but feels powerless to do anything to change the situation. In her mind she is the victim of parents who haven't used wise judgment. In reality, it is her unforgiving heart that causes her to feel the way she does.

She can change this by choosing to forgive her parents, regardless of whether or not they change. This power was given to her when she accepted Jesus as her Savior, but she must choose to utilize it.

Think of a shiny, brand-new toaster sitting on your counter. Unless you press the lever that causes it to begin toasting, it won't work, even though it is capable of doing so.

Carol is much like that toaster. She has the power to forgive, but she isn't activating it. An unforgiving heart is a heavy weight to carry. It will affect everyone around you, especially your husband, for the marriage relationship generally bears the brunt of an unforgiving heart in either partner. A woman will not be a helper to her husband when she is absorbed in recounting others' offenses toward her. Unless you avail yourself of God's power to forgive freely, you'll find yourself hashing out anoth-

A woman will not be a helper to her husband when she is absorbed in recounting others' offenses toward her.

er's offense toward you over and over again. When you don't forgive, the tendency to dwell on things is stronger than the tendency to forgive. You must choose forgiveness in order to get on with your life, and in order to glorify God.

Is this happening in your marriage? Do you find yourself reliving how another has wronged you? If so, reconcile this issue today. How? Ask God to forgive you for your unforgiving heart. Then choose to forgive that person for his or her offense toward you. Perhaps it would help to talk with a pastor or a godly friend. You'll be amazed to discover how forgiving others clears the way for you to be a helper to your husband in the way God intended.

PRINCIPLE 2: FORGIVENESS IS LIMITLESS

Do you ever tire of forgiving? Do you feel that you have done more than your fair share in this area? Have you set up a mental checklist of prerequisites that must be met in order for you to offer forgiveness to another? Is there a limit on how many times you are required to forgive another? Jesus answered those questions in a conversation He had with Peter, who was refreshingly honest when he asked Jesus, "Lord, how many times shall I forgive my brother when he sins against me? Up to seven times?" (Matthew 18:21).

Don't we also do that as wives? We forgive our husbands a number of times, but when their forgiveness quotient is used up, rather than continuing to forgive, we begin keeping a record of their mistakes, forgetting that love doesn't take into account a wrong suffered (1 Corinthians 13:5). We do this with others as well. We draw an imaginary line in the sand, and once that line is crossed, we are through forgiving.

But this isn't God's way of doing things! Listen to what He says to Peter: "I tell you, not seven times, but seventy-seven times" (Matthew 18:22).

In other words, He says we are to forgive over and over again. *Stop counting and start forgiving.*

Often a wife finds it easier to forgive her husband the first few times he offends than after he's done something for the umpteenth time. The husband of a friend of ours has a habit of becoming short-tempered and agitated when he's hot or tired. They live in the South, and he has a highly stressful job, so the opportunities for him to be irritable are limitless! And often he takes full advantage of those opportunities. His behavior is wearying to her, and at times she finds herself reluctant to forgive him one more time for the same irritation. "Why can't he see what he's doing and change?" she wonders. "I've told him often enough." She has discovered, however, that when she withholds forgiveness, she is the one most miserable.

When you don't forgive, you are effectively saying, "I no longer want to be like Christ." Of course, that is never the place of blessing. Our passion should be to dwell in that blessed place! For our friend, it is this simple yet powerful thought that spurs her, as it should us, to forgive her husband over and over again.

Many times basic personality differences are the kindling for a raging fire of harsh words, snide remarks, and flippant behavior. In fact these things sometimes happen many times in the course of one day.

In his study guide, *Discover Your Giftedness in Christ,* Dr. Mels Carbonell profiles four models of human behavior based on temperament.[1] My (Nancy) husband is at one end of the scale and tends to be direct, decisive, determined, and driven. I land toward the other end, and my temperament is almost the direct opposite of my husband's. For a long time I wondered, "Why can't Ray be more like me? Then we'd be so happy!" What seemed like common sense to me at the time was nothing more than pride.

It was life changing to discover that what I was holding against him was intrinsic to his God-given personality. Before long I realized that what I actually would not forgive was his *personality!*

Look at your own relationship. Are your personality differences one of the reasons for discord in your marriage? This is a form of lovelessness and reveals a judgmental spirit. A wise woman understands the way her husband is wired and accepts him for who he is. God complements and balances a couple through their differences.

When problems crop up in your marriage, remember that forgiveness is limitless. Choose to honor God by forgiving easily and often.

PRINCIPLE 3: FORGIVENESS OF OTHERS SHOULD MIRROR GOD'S FORGIVENESS OF YOU

Matthew 18:21–35 clearly illustrates this principle. Jesus spoke of a servant who owed a king ten thousand talents, a vast sum of money. The servant was unable to repay the king, so the king ordered that the servant, his wife, his children, and all that he had be sold to repay the debt. Everything he had, *including his family,* was to be sold in order to repay the king.

But the servant fell on his knees before the king and begged, "Be patient with me, and I will pay back everything."

The king took pity on him, canceled the debt, and let him go. He didn't merely adjust the debt or give the servant more time to come up with the money. He canceled the debt in full.

The forgiven man left and soon came upon a fellow servant who owed him a hundred denarii, or about a hundred days' wages. This was pittance, compared to what he had owed the king. Yet he grabbed his fellow servant and began choking him. "'Pay back what you owe me!' he demanded" (v. 28).

His fellow servant fell to his knees and begged him, "Be patient with me, and I will pay you back." (v. 29)

What a perfect opportunity for the servant to follow the king's gracious example by extending that same grace to another. But instead he refused to forgive the meager debt and had the man thrown into prison until he could repay what he owed. He didn't offer to adjust or cancel the debt, but chose to take swift, harsh action.

When the other servants saw what happened, they were greatly disturbed and reported to the king everything that had taken place.

What do you think the king did when he heard the news? It would seem natural that he would rush to the jail and release the imprisoned man. But that's not what happened. Instead, he called the unforgiving man in for a conference.

Not mincing words, he said, "You wicked servant…I canceled all that debt of yours because you begged me to. Shouldn't you have had mercy on your fellow servant just as I had on you?" (vv.

32–33). In anger, the king turned him over to the jailers to be put in prison *and tortured* until he paid back all he owed.

Did you notice that the unforgiving man was put into prison for nonpayment of debt? *The very thing he wouldn't forgive came back into his own life.*

Jesus tells us that if we pardon and release (give up resentment and let it drop), we will be pardoned and released: "Do not judge, and you will not be judged. Do not condemn, and you will not be condemned. Forgive, and you will be forgiven" (Luke 6:37).

Did you notice that the unforgiving servant in this parable was put into prison *and tortured?* He was in the same position as the man he had just refused to forgive, but worse. He was imprisoned and tortured until he paid back all that he owed. The huge debt that the king was once willing to cancel was back on him. The "forgotten" debt was remembered and would not be dropped until payment was made in full. The story ends with a riveting statement: "This is how my heavenly Father will treat each of you unless you forgive your brother from your heart" (Matthew 18:35).

Unless we forgive our brother from our heart! This passage reveals that unforgivingness actually affects how Christ will treat us.

The city where we live has garbage collection once a week. On one occasion, due to a snowstorm, my (Connie) family didn't take the trash to the curb in time to be picked up. By the next week, we had trash spilling everywhere.

When you forgive quickly, bitterness isn't allowed to make its nest in your heart.

When you don't forgive others in a timely manner, your heart begins spilling over with garbage called bitterness. When you forgive quickly, bitterness isn't allowed to make its nest in your heart. When you choose otherwise, the underpinnings for bitterness are established. Forgiveness invites God to pour out His blessings on your life. Unforgivingness invites Him to do the opposite.

Did you realize that when you are disobedient to God's Word, He will allow pressures to come into your life to press you back to Himself? These could include depression, frustration, bitterness, or even illness brought on by stress. He may be pressing you right now to forgive, as He did with a young woman we know whose life, including her marriage, was affected by bitterness.

The Less Loved Daughter

There is a second story about a less loved daughter, but this one has a different outcome. This woman's father had two daughters. For whatever reason, the father preferred the older daughter, and the younger child felt it. A day came when she confronted her dad about this. He denied it, but it was true. Most everyone who knew the family noticed the favoritism, but the father refused to acknowledge it.

The father died with the issue unresolved, and in the following years the younger daughter grew increasingly depressed about her feelings toward her deceased dad.

One day she heard this specific teaching on forgiveness. As she walked to her car afterward, she realized that she had never forgiven her father for showing favoritism to her sister. She could see that she was "imprisoned with torture."

As she got into her car and prepared to drive away, she decided it was time to face the facts. She drove straight to the cemetery and stood before her father's grave. There, alone, surrounded by her memories and her sorrow, she took action.

She asked God to forgive her unforgivingness toward her father. Then she directed her attention to his grave and said, "Dad, I forgive you." She later told a friend that at that moment the heavy burden she had been carrying was gone, laid to rest once and for all. It was a turning point in her life.

If someone has hurt you and it has become an issue between you and that person, it would be most appropriate to resolve the issue face-to-face. Many times, though, the other person is unaware of the way you feel. If that's the case, prayerfully consider forgiving him or her without the other person's knowledge.

We could give numerous examples of the freedom that forgiveness brings, but we are limited by the constraints of time and space. However, the one question we encourage you to ask yourself is this: *Are there people in my life, now or in the past, that I've never forgiven?* If there are, forgive them, and then ask God's forgiveness for your unforgiving heart.

Of course, many problems are not caused by a woman's lack of forgiveness. A problem may exist in your marriage because of the willful disobedience of your spouse or others. God will deal with their disobedience. Your responsibility is to walk in obedience to Him regardless of another's actions.

The Parable Concludes

At the conclusion of Jesus' parable, both men were imprisoned. The king never did release the servant who owed the meager debt, although we might have hoped He would. But he did take action against the man who refused to give others what he himself had been given.

The parallel for us is that Christ died on the cross to forgive our sins. He forgave us a huge debt, our lifetime of sin, which is represented by the ten thousand talents the first servant owed the king. What He asks in return is for us to forgive others.

It was the predetermined plan and foreknowledge of God *that Jesus' death on the cross would accomplish forgiveness for our sins* (Acts 2:23). Apart from His death, there would be no forgiveness and we would be separated eternally from God. But because of Jesus' death, we can look forward to spending eternity with Him if we've trusted Him as our Savior.

Prior to His crucifixion, Jesus was seized and arrested in the Garden of Gethsemane. He was beaten, flogged, and taunted. A crown of thorns was placed upon His head, and He was nailed to the cross. And there on Calvary's hill, before the Lamb of God died, all of our sins, which He was literally dying to forgive, came upon Him. The minute—the *instant*—He gave up His spirit and died, forgiveness was achieved (John 1:29; 1 Corinthians 15:3; 2 Corinthians 5:21; Revelation 1:5).

Once you put your trust in Christ, your salvation is never lost, but you can choose to live in the prison of unforgivingness. Galatians 5:1 says that you are set free for freedom! Why would you ever choose to give up your freedom through unforgivingness? The price is so high, the payment so costly:

> You were not redeemed with perishable things like silver or gold…but with precious blood, as of a lamb unblemished and spotless, the blood of Christ. (1 Peter 1:18–19, NASB)

Don't hold your gift of freedom lightly. It cost Jesus everything!

PRINCIPLE 4: FORGIVENESS IS YOUR BIRTHRIGHT

Are you extremely hard on yourself, especially in the area of for-giveness? Have you caused another a great deal of pain or sadness? Were you raised in a home where forgiveness was extended reluc-tantly, if at all? Perhaps, then, you have a difficult time receiving for-giveness from others and from God as well. You can forgive everyone else, but you won't forgive yourself.

If you are such a person, remember that *Jesus died on the cross for your sins.* They have been washed away…cleansed…covered. If you ask for His forgiveness, you receive it instantly. Accept it! *He has already given it to you.* It is your birthright as a member of God's family. To not receive forgiveness, or to convince yourself that you aren't worthy of it, is to say that Christ's death wasn't enough.

We know of a man who as a young adult killed numerous people. He lived a life far removed from what most of us could ever imagine. Eventually he turned away from that life and began searching for something to hold on to. His despair only deepened, however, because he was haunted by his past. One day a stranger told him about the saving grace of Jesus Christ and how His death on the cross covered all his sins.

"But you don't understand my sins," the man cried out. "How can God forgive me when I can't forgive myself?"

"You don't understand my Savior," the stranger replied. "Every single one of your sins, however heinous, has been washed clean by His blood." After further conversation, the man trusted Jesus to be his Savior. The healing process began, and a sense of peace enveloped him.

Whatever it is you're hanging on to, it's time to let it go. Psalm

147:3 tells us that "He heals the brokenhearted and binds up their wounds." Allow Jesus to heal your heartaches. Open the door to His peace.

All too often we project our own personality onto God. This is especially true of a person who forgives slowly. We think He is like us. *But He is not!* We don't have to perform prolonged acts of penance to receive His forgiveness, for no condemnation hangs over the heads of those who are His. The judge Himself has declared us free from sin. You are acceptable because of what Jesus did on the cross. You don't have to do anything to earn God's forgiveness, except confess your sin to Him. There is no reason to sink down into regret, shame, or denial or make excuses for what you've done. Simply tell Him and thank Him for His grace.

A wise woman keeps short accounts with the Lord through a daily time of confession. He is faithful to His word, and He promises instant forgiveness. First John 1:9 tells us that "if we confess our sins, he is faithful and just and will forgive us our sins and purify us from all unrighteousness."

Jesus demonstrated this very thing when He washed his disciples' feet. He said that "he who has bathed needs only to wash his feet, but is completely clean" (John 13:10, NASB). If a person takes a bath then walks barefoot into the yard to get the evening newspaper, he needs only to wash the grass and dust from his feet before going to bed. Spiritually, when you ask Jesus to be your Savior, you have been cleansed from sin, as in taking a bath. However, you will sin from time to time. To be completely clean again, all you need to do is confess these sins before Jesus.

Not having a daily confession time results in feeling unclean and perhaps guilty. Never forget that guilt is a friend that takes you to the cross; once you have confessed your sins, its work is finished. If you continue to feel guilty over a sin that has been confessed, that feeling is not from God. There is nothing in your past that Jesus' death didn't cover. Nothing.

PRINCIPLE 5: FORGIVENESS IS A CHOICE

It is a simple yet powerful realization that forgiveness is a choice. You can choose to forgive out of obedience to Christ regardless of your feelings. If forgiveness were dependent on our feelings, we might never forgive. Jesus' feelings had nothing to do with His obedience to His Father. Remember, He prayed, "My Father, if it is possible, let this cup pass from Me; yet not as I will, but as Thou wilt" (Matthew 26:39, NASB). Ultimately, one's life is based on the choices one makes. Forgiving others is *always* the right choice.

When you purchase a car, you must decide which options you want. Do you want leather seats, sporty hubcaps, or four-wheel drive? In some cars, even the floor mats are optional.

Forgiveness isn't an option in a godly marriage; it is a must. It was meant to be standard equipment for the godly wife. Forgiveness puts the pieces back in place when they've been broken apart or blown to bits; it is the very cement that glues the heart together. Learning to forgive your mate for his shortcomings and oversights is critical if you want to become the wife God intended you to be.

When we (Connie) were first married, if my husband said anything that was critical or abrupt, I forgave him instantly. Many times I forgave him whether he asked for my forgiveness or not, so eager was I to keep the channels of love and communication open. As the years went by, however, my eagerness dimmed, and that instant forgiveness ceased to exist. I found myself feeling annoyed at little things, such as the way he squeezed the toothpaste or hung his towel. I had gone from a wife who quickly forgave to a wife who rarely forgave.

In short, I had become a full-time bookkeeper. I kept a record of everything my husband did that annoyed me. Or irritated me. Or frustrated me. I kept detailed accounts of all the things I did for him and all the things I thought he should be doing for me, but wasn't. I kept mental notes each time my feelings were hurt. I was extremely busy, and my accounting business was thriving, but my marriage was not.

As I grew in spiritual maturity, I would attempt to reconcile the records. I would forgive my husband, wipe the slate clean, and commit to starting over again. This would last anywhere from a few days to a few weeks, when, for whatever reason, I would feel offended once again. At that point I would reopen my accounting business and be busier than ever updating the files. How I had changed from the early days of my marriage, when my husband's happiness had meant the world to me!

Like thousands of other women, I always wondered why my marriage ran so hot and cold. For me the root of this cycle was the lack of true, instead of temporary, forgiveness. Temporary forgiveness does not exist. To forgive temporarily is not really to forgive.

My grandmother used to say, "No matter what happens to me in life, I hope I will always remember who I am." She thought she could handle almost anything except losing her mental capabilities.

When I heard her say this, I would think, *No matter what happens to me in life, I hope I never turn into a bitter woman.* As a young girl, I found it fascinating to watch women and study what made them tick. I noticed that as a woman aged, she frequently seemed to become bitter and joyless. It was rare to find an older woman whose heart was joyful.

I was surprised and saddened to realize, at the ripe old age of thirty-five, that I had become the woman I hoped never to resemble. It was only when I understood this principle of forgiveness, *and chose to forgive,* that I was able, by God's grace, to move forward in this area.

PRINCIPLE 6: FORGIVENESS LEAVES THE CONSEQUENCES TO GOD

Choosing to forgive an offense doesn't mean there aren't consequences for the offender, just that they don't come from our hand. The Bible instructs us to leave the consequences up to God:

> Never take your own revenge, beloved, but leave room for the wrath of God, for it is written, "VENGEANCE IS MINE, I WILL REPAY," says the Lord. (Romans 12:19, NASB)

The consequences are to be decided by God, not us. Refusing to take them into our own hands will clear the way for Him to deal with the offender. "Do not gloat when your enemy falls; when he stumbles, do not let your heart rejoice, or the LORD will see and disapprove and turn his wrath away from him" (Proverbs 24:17–18).

PRINCIPLE 7: FORGIVENESS COLORS EVERYTHING

When I (Connie) was a young girl, I used to help my mother make angel food cakes from scratch. It seemed we beat those egg whites forever before they were just right. Once the batter was made, Mom would pour some of it into another bowl. Then she'd take a drop of red food coloring and make that batter pink. My sisters and I loved seeing the cake come out of the oven with a pink ring in the center. It never ceased to amaze me that one tiny drop could color an entire bowl of batter.

Similarly, when you choose to forgive, every area of your life is affected. Your thought life changes, and you no longer obsess over who did what to whom. Not only does it alter the way you interact with the person involved; it most likely changes how you interact with others as well.

Forgiveness fosters growth in your Christian life and fine-tunes your prayer life. It can literally change your appearance, improve your sleeping habits, and give you a renewed zest for life. Some people believe it is instrumental in relieving certain types of depression. It may also bring about reconciliation and resurrect dead or dying relationships. Forgiveness removes the heavy padlock of unforgivingness from your heart; your life will bear witness to this in many ways.

Not long ago a friend told us that two members of her family hadn't spoken in almost twenty years due to differences of opinion regarding some farmland. Their farms adjoined one another, and their paths crossed frequently, yet nary a word had passed between them since the dispute. The entire community was aware of the unfortunate situation.

One afternoon one of the women picked up the phone and called the other. "May I come over for a while tonight? I'd like to speak with you."

"Yes, you certainly may," the other replied.

The two women met that night. After a few awkward moments, the first said, "I'm not even sure what happened way back then, but whatever it was, I'd like to ask your forgiveness." The other woman concurred. Since that day, the two have shared a close relationship. As one woman commented, "Forgiveness touched everything in my life. Even my food tastes better!"

Did you notice how the first woman took the initiative in seeking forgiveness? This is key and is the most mature thing we can do as Christian women. We must take the initiative in resolving conflicts.

Forgiveness colors and enriches every aspect of life. *And so does unforgivingness.* When you choose to forgive, you'll discover how God blesses a forgiving spirit. But He *cannot and will not* bless an unforgiving one. Won't you, today, allow the beautiful hue of forgiveness to color your life?

CLARIFICATIONS

From our own personal experiences and from talking with women, we've discovered that forgiveness is often seen through a distorted lens, which causes confusion and uncertainty. Below is a clarification of what forgiveness does not necessarily entail:

1. Forgiveness doesn't always mean reconciliation. In order for reconciliation to occur, trust must be reestablished. This

requires cooperation and true repentance from the offender. Since the actions of another are essential for reconciliation, there is no guarantee that this will happen.

2. Forgiving isn't necessarily forgetting. How often have we heard the phrase "forgive and forget"? To forgive others as God forgave us implies forgetting. This should be our goal; however, in our human state we will often remember the event and the resulting pain. But we can refuse to let these memories cripple, embitter, or weaken our faith. You might be surprised to find that the memory of the offense fades over time.

3. Forgiving isn't excusing or tolerating. You aren't required to make excuses for another's poor behavior (they didn't know better, they didn't have the advantages I had, they practically raised themselves). Everyone is responsible before God for his or her actions and may well suffer consequences as a result of them.

   Take the initiative in seeking forgiveness.

4. Forgiveness isn't dependent upon another's acceptance of it. There may be times when you forgive someone, but he or she refuses to accept your forgiveness. This doesn't negate the sincerity of your forgiveness in any way.

5. Forgiving isn't making certain that others forgive you. You can seek forgiveness from others, but whether they choose to give it or not is up to them. *You aren't responsible for another's forgiveness.* Don't allow this to emotionally imprison you.

CHRIST'S FINAL WORDS TO ANOTHER

Before dying on the cross, Christ's final words to another human being were words of forgiveness. Luke tells us of this last precious conversation between a mortal man—a thief, no less—and the immortal Christ.

> One of the criminals who hung there hurled insults at him: "Aren't you the Christ? Save yourself and us!"
>
> But the other criminal rebuked him. "Don't you fear God," he said, "since you are under the same sentence? We are punished justly, for we are getting what our deeds deserve. But this man has done nothing wrong."
>
> Then he said, "Jesus, remember me when you come into your kingdom."
>
> Jesus answered him, "I tell you the truth, today you will be with me in paradise." (Luke 23:39–43)

The thief saw with his own eyes, from his unique vantage point, Jesus dying on the cross, bleeding from all He had endured. Yet the thief realized that this was the Son of God and believed that He would come into His kingdom. Amazingly, the thief came to a decision in the very last moments of his life, asking Christ to remember him in His resurrection.

After all He had endured—the betrayals, the beatings, the floggings, the spitting, the insults—Jesus heard the thief and responded with open arms.

With gentleness and compassion, He said to him, "I tell you the truth, today you will be with me in paradise." The thief, in his final few moments of life, was forgiven.

We often want to forgive, but only if it comes easily, especially in our marriages. If it is a difficult situation or the circumstances are especially hurtful, we want to step back, nurse our wounds, and think it over. Christ didn't do that. He didn't step back. Instead, He allowed His feet to be nailed to a cross. He didn't nurse His wounds, and they were far deeper and more painful than yours or ours. He thought over only one thing: whether or not He was doing the will of His Father.

How long has it been since you've considered doing God's will regarding forgiving another? His desire is for you to forgive. Over and over and over again. Are you a forgiving person? Would you consider following God's plan for your life in this area?

The hallmark of Jesus' life was forgiveness.

It's the reason He was born.

It's the reason He lived.

It's the reason He died.

Is forgiveness a hallmark of your life? Through Christ, you can forgive others and you can humbly ask others to forgive you. And you can know that by doing so, you are becoming more and more like Jesus!

Chapter Four: What Makes Your Heart Beat Faster?

A few years ago, my (Connie) aunt suffered a massive stroke. Because I lived just a few hours away, I decided to drive to the hospital to be with the family for a day.

The city was large and unfamiliar to me. I became lost and found myself in a remote, deserted area. My three-year-old daughter was with me, and I was nervous and afraid.

Finally, after several blocks, I drove out of that section of town, and there in front of me stood the hospital for which I was searching. My muscles relaxed, and relief flooded my body.

I visited with my cousins, and that evening when it came time to leave, I dreaded the prospect of finding my way back to the interstate. "Stay close to us," my cousins said. "We'll lead you to the interstate."

I stayed so close to them they thought our bumpers were connected! There was no way I was going to let them out of my sight. Because of their leading, my return trip was easy.

Staying close to my cousins altered my trip home. What do you suppose would happen if we stayed close to our King?

This is called abiding, and there's nothing else like it on earth! You'll find your relationship with Jesus to be more intimate when you do this, and you'll discover a peace and contentment you didn't have before. And your trip "home" will be far richer as well!

Abiding in Christ—are you close to your King?

What Makes Your Heart Beat Faster?

Abiding is the heartbeat of the Christian walk.

ome. The very word should bring to your mind a sense of security and peace. It is a place that you can retreat to and be revived. The ideal home is where you experience another's unconditional love and undivided attention. The welcome mat is always at the door, and even as you approach you can almost see arms opened wide to embrace you.

When we have family and friends visit, we make an extra effort to show them our love. The guest room is made ready with handmade quilts on the bed and extras nearby in case they need additional warmth. We might set out a tray that holds a teapot and teacups and perhaps a vase with fresh flowers. Along with this, we make sure plenty of reading material is available—a daily devotional, books of interest, perhaps a new magazine or two.

I (Nancy) have a tall tree decorated with little white lights that stands in the corner of my guest room. At night I draw a bath for my loved one. I have a tray that stretches across the tub, and on it

I place lighted candles and a cup of tea. A pillow to rest the head on is at the back of the tub, and nearby is a small tape recorder, which plays soft music. We often give our guests inexpensive items that will serve as a reminder of our time together. This attention to their comfort touches them, and it delights us when we are privileged to welcome guests into our home.

We can, for a day or two, bring refreshment to another—but being at home in Christ is to be cared for twenty-four hours a day, year-round.

You cannot be a helper to your husband the way God intended apart from abiding in Christ. Abiding impacts everything in your life—not just your marriage, but everything! When you focus on Christ instead of on your husband, something inexplicable and marvelous happens to you. Your role as helper becomes not only possible; it becomes thrilling as well!

Jesus says when you come to Him, you will find
rest…
    relief…
        ease…
            refreshment…
                recreation…
                    and blessed quiet for your souls.
                    (Matthew 11:28–29, AMP)

I (Nancy) have visited some of the great homes of the world. I've stood in front of the White House in Washington, D.C., but those who lived there didn't welcome me in as their guest. When I walked by the Palace of the Emperor in Tokyo, Japan, I wasn't even noticed. As I visited Buckingham Palace in London, to my amazement, Queen Elizabeth and her husband rode by in a horse-drawn carriage. She even waved to me. But she did not stop to invite me in. There is a royal home, however, where the door is not only open, but where you are invited to be forever.

A ROYAL HOME

Did you know that you can have a permanent place in a royal home? You can. Jesus Himself initiates this most intimate relationship with Him. Jesus freely gives this home to those who have responded to His initial call, "Come and follow Me." He says, "Abide in Me, live in Me, make your home in Me, just as I do in you" (John 15:4, paraphrased).

When you come home to Him, you will find what you have been looking for all your life. When you are at home in Christ, you experience His wholehearted love and complete attention. He notices your weariness. He sees when you are heavy laden and overburdened. When the worries of the world seem to overwhelm you, He is always ready to comfort and strengthen you.

When you are at home in Christ, you will find what you've been looking for all your life.

A. W. Tozer speaks of this abiding faith walk as "the gaze of the soul on God."[1] Perhaps you have seen a field of sunflowers at a point in the day when their faces are pointed upward, basking in the warmth of the sun. They are not pointed downward or sideways, but stand fully upright, open wide to the heavens. When our hearts are like that, basking in His radiance and glory, longing to do what pleases Him, we are *abiding*.

To abide means to stay in the same place with the same person. It is a life of sweet companionship with Christ. Abiding is an interactive partnership between Almighty God and a believer. An abider depends on God and focuses on His strength, His sufficiency, and His enabling power.

In his book *Daily with the King,* W. Glyn Evans says that abiding is described as three things:

> A conscious awareness of His presence at all times. That does not mean direct verbal communication with Him, but the feeling that He is there, as a child playing is aware of its mother's nearby presence.
>
> Second, it also means a careful consultation with Him about everything that affects us. That consultation may be in direct prayer, or else in scanning the Bible indirectly for any message He has for us there. The important thing is to keep the lines of communication open with Him so that we are instantly ready to receive any necessary message sent from Him.
>
> Third, it means a continual enjoyment of Him as a person. That means He is a joy, a delight to us at all times; the very thought of Him fills us with pleasure.[2]

This abiding relationship is open to all believers, but many are uncertain how they can have it. Sadly, many who do understand this principle are unwilling to give what Jesus requires.

THE COST

"If you keep My commandments, you will abide in My love; just as I have kept My Father's commandments and abide in His love." (John 15:10, NASB)

The requirement for abiding is obedience to the Father. That is how you remain in fellowship with Christ. That is also the way to walk as He walked, which is what we are challenged to do: "The one who says he abides in Him ought himself to walk in the same manner as He walked" (1 John 2:6, NASB).

Obedience is submission to the authority of God. As you read your Bible, do you apply what you are learning to your own life? When you see areas in your life that need to change, do you commit to changing them, or do you instead try to figure out reasons to continue living as you are?

The requirement for abiding is obedience to the Father.

Do you recall wanting your own way when you were a small child and how your parents tried to keep you from the dangers that might have resulted if you had gotten it? "Don't run into the street!" "Don't talk to strangers!" "Don't touch the oven, the plug, the spider..." Sometimes they told you why, and other times they just said, "Don't!"

I (Nancy) can remember my own father's instructions: "Nan, don't do such and so," he would tell me. Always, I would ask why. Sometimes he would tell me, and other times he'd simply say, "Because I have a reason."

There is always a perfect reason to be obedient to God.

Sometimes the answer is obvious; other times we choose to obey simply because God said so, even though His reasons may be unclear.

I (Connie) was a Christian for many years before I began to understand the principle of abiding. Prior to that, I thought abiding was about a few verses in the Bible rather than an ongoing, intimate walk with Jesus. But one day I finally got it. It became crystal clear, as when a lens suddenly focuses. It was then that I fully understood that the cost of abiding was obedience.

And I was so disappointed! I felt weary—and I had just begun. To me *obedience* was a plodding kind of word. It reminded me of a workhorse toiling along in the field, with endless acres of soil to turn. Row after row the horse trudges, straining to pull the heavy plow. I am grieved to admit this, but that is how I felt.

Only later, as I began to practice obedience, did I discover how sorely mistaken I had been. Obedience isn't a plodding kind of thing. It isn't trudging along, as I had thought. *Obedience is what frees you to run!* It is the very thing that brings you into a warm, close relationship with Jesus. Once you discover the sweet taste of obedience, you will no longer want to settle for less.

So often we want to experience the blessings of obedience without obeying. We want fulfilled marriages without being excellent wives. We want personal satisfaction and joy, but we want the option of dragging our heels whenever we feel like it. We want to know God's will for our lives, but we're too busy to sit at His feet and discover just what that is. Many want to be godly, but few are willing to be obedient. Yet obedience is the very thing on which abiding hinges. Obedience opens the door to an understanding of who God is and shows us more and more fully what His will for our lives is.

God instructed Noah to build an ark of enormous proportions in an era that had yet to see rain. This was no small project. The building project took over one hundred years and was done during a time when the wickedness of man was great. But Noah abided in the presence of God—in fact, the Bible says he *walked* with God. His faith was deep long *before* the flood. Noah's task was major and lengthy, but he carried it out because God had told Him to, even though it may have seemed an odd command at the time. In essence, it was Noah's personal obedience to God's word that saved not only himself, *but his family as well.* After the rains and the flooding, they were the only humans on earth. Your presence on this earth bears witness to Noah's obedience.

The place of abiding is where you experience the reality of God's fathomless love. Andrew Murray says, "Abiding in Jesus is nothing but the giving up of oneself to be ruled and taught and led, and so resting in the arms of Everlasting Love."[3]

We have a friend who lived a seemingly successful, fulfilling life. In his late forties he was a successful businessman who was widely respected. Recently, however, he felt a restlessness in his spirit and sensed a void in his life. One day he approached a man in his office that he knew to be a Christian even though he wasn't sure what that meant. "There's got to be more to life than what I'm experiencing," he told the man. "I have everything I ever thought I could want, yet something is missing. Can you teach me about the Bible?"

Of course, the man in his office was more than happy to do this! He told our friend about Jesus, and our friend made the decision to ask Him to be his personal Savior, which is the first step to abiding. In that instant, his life was changed! He began to pray and ask God to reveal Himself to him. Yearning to know more about his Savior, he became active in a Bible study. He began spending time with God and found a peace that he had never before known. Now not only does he reside in a lovely earthly residence, but he also abides in a place far more beautiful: a royal home that gives him what his earthly home cannot. He is now *at home* in Christ.

THE PLUMB LINE

If you've ever hung wallpaper, you know that one of the first things you do is put up a plumb line. This is a piece of string with a weight at one end. You nail this weighted cord to the seam where the ceiling meets the wall. Then you put the first sheet of wallpaper exactly where the cord is hanging. By doing this, you ensure that the wallpaper will be straight.

The plumb line for your life is the Word of God. When your behavior is lined up with what God reveals in the Bible, you become straight with God. This is called obedience, and it is the front door to abiding. There is no other entrance.

Years ago, as a new Christian, all of this talk about obedience surprised me (Nancy). I remember thinking I'd have to give up many of the things I enjoyed. One was a "hobby" I had stumbled into called anger.

This hobby was thriving when I learned that the sun shouldn't go down on my anger (Ephesians 4:26). My walk with Christ was so new that my first thought was, *What fun is that?* I wasn't sure I could do it since anger had become such a big part of me. If someone hurt my feelings, I would become withdrawn and quiet until they seemed sorry enough for the offense. Because of my desire to abide in Christ, I set a goal: to get over my anger by sundown each day. I would actually peer out the window to see how much time I had left before I had to give up my anger. Just as the sun was disappearing for the day, I would force myself to forgive the person. As the weeks went by, this seemed more trouble than it was worth. I soon began forgiving more and more quickly—even in the daylight! I couldn't believe the freedom my obedience brought me. I experienced Christ's love for me in a deeper way and felt it increasingly as I began obeying in other areas of my life.

THE OUTCOME

Jesus says that when you abide in Him and in His love, the outcome will be joy. His actual words are: "My joy may be in you, and that your joy may be made full" (John 15:11, NASB).

Are you joyful? If not, do you now know why? *His joy is extended to abiders.* Abiders are obeyers; obeyers are choosers. They choose to do what God says. They place their faith in Him as Noah did, regardless of whether they fully understand the command or feel like doing it at the moment.

What are the results of faith in God, of coming to the Father through Jesus?

Obedience grows out of love for Jesus and His word.

This opens the door to abiding,

which is the foundation for experiencing

His peace...

His love...

His joy! (John 14:21, 27; 15:9, 11)

Fruitfulness

Jesus goes on to say that as you abide in Him, you will bear fruit:

> "As the branch cannot bear fruit of itself unless it abides in
> the vine, so neither can you unless you abide in Me. I am
> the vine, you are the branches; he who abides in Me and I
> in him, he bears much fruit, for apart from Me you can do
> nothing." (John 15:4–5, NASB)

Fruit is the outcome of your obedience to Christ, and it is dependent on your choice to abide. "The fruit of the Spirit is love, joy, peace, patience, kindness, goodness, faithfulness, gentleness and self-control" (Galatians 5:22–23). As you learn to abide more and more in Christ, the fruitbearing in your life will be greater.

He is the vine; you are the branch. You cannot bear fruit apart from Him, just as a branch cannot bear fruit apart from the vine.

Stop reading for a moment and think about this. It is one of the most profound truths in Scripture, and it affects all that you are and all that you do. *Apart from Christ you have no power to live a victorious life.*

The friend we mentioned earlier bore lots of earthly fruit from his labors, but he bore no spiritual fruit before he asked Jesus to be his Savior. He couldn't, for he was living apart from Christ.

Are you availing yourself of the power Jesus so freely offers? Do you know how to activate that power? *It is a simple thing to do.* If a fan isn't plugged in, it is unable to circulate air, for it has no power apart from the electricity that powers it. It works only after it's plugged into an electrical source.

Similarly, if you aren't abiding in Christ, you may have salvation through Him, but you have no power to be fruitful and joyful. With Him living in you, and you in Him, you have all the power and resources you need to do this, not only in your marriage, but in the rest of your life as well. Christ is in you constantly through the presence of the Holy Spirit. This is what is meant by the Spirit-filled life.

Abiding in Christ is the only way to be a Christlike woman and wife. We cannot overemphasize the simplicity and reality of this promise. If you don't grasp this partnership, you will become discouraged because you will have no strength to live a victorious life.

Warren and Ruth Myers said, "We find a night and day difference in our lives when we choose against struggling to be strong and peaceful and loving—and instead, count on the strength and peace and love of Christ's life within us."[4]

Hudson Taylor, a famous missionary to China, struggled to abide. One day he received a letter from John McCarthy. One particular sentence from McCarthy's letter removed the scales from his eyes: "But how to get faith strengthened? Not by striving after faith, but by resting on the Faithful One." "Ah, there is rest!" Taylor thought. "I have striven in vain to rest in Him. I'll strive no more. For has He not promised to abide with me—never to leave me, never to fail me?"[5]

So often, we try to perform the work of the Spirit ourselves. We live in an age that says if we just work hard enough, we can accomplish anything. But we will never accomplish something that God Himself was meant to do. *He* is the vine; we are the branches. As we cling to *Him,* He produces the fruit in us.

My (Connie) family always had a vegetable garden, and my sisters and I spent time tending it. One of our jobs was to pick the ripened red tomatoes. Sometimes, though, we'd accidentally hit a green tomato that wasn't ready to be picked. If we hit it hard enough to jar it loose from the vine, it no longer received nourishment and withered and died.

That's the idea here. When we allow ourselves to become detached or loosened from His Word through disobedience, fruit is no longer produced in our lives. Our salvation is still assured, but there is no fruit.

YOUR PART

What is your part in abiding? You need to depend on and surrender to Jesus Christ:

> *Dependence:* Looking to Him, trusting Him for present power, resting in His love.
>
> *Surrender:* Acknowledging that you can do *nothing* apart from Him and that you need His help and power.

Too often we think that trying harder is the answer to our problems—that it will dissolve the roadblocks and barriers in our marriage and in life in general. I (Connie) did this for years. On my good days, I was willing to try harder; on my bad days, I expected my husband to. But trying harder isn't the answer, because *you* aren't the source of power that is needed for a changed life. *Christ* is, and His working in you through the Holy Spirit.

Returning to the example of the fan, your trying harder would be like plugging the fan into an electrical outlet that is dead. From all outward appearances, the fan ought to work, but it never will because there is no power available to cause the fan to whirl to life. You can turn the switch on as often as you like, but the fan will remain motionless until it's plugged into a true source of power.

Similarly, you can continue trying harder for as long as you like, but nothing will happen because there is no real power from which to draw. You're relying on yourself for power that only Christ can give. Fruit will be produced in your life only as you draw from Christ's strength instead of from your own. You simply cooperate through obedience.

How can you get in the habit of being aware that Christ is in you and with you? How can you begin cooperating through obedience? An excellent way to begin is with prayer, because abiding is the prerequisite for effective prayer.

PRAYER

"If you abide in Me, and My words abide in you, ask whatever you wish, and it will be done for you" (John 15:7, NASB). Abiding encourages us to ask Jesus for anything. In their book *31 Days of Prayer,* Ruth and Warren Myers say:

> As your hand experiences the life of your body as its own, so as you abide in Christ you experience the life of Christ as your own. Life that is fresh, pure, joyous, fruitful, free of anxiety, and full of faith. Life that is wrapped up in the desires that are in God's heart. Then when you pray, you express His longings; you want what He wants. And so He does what you ask.[6]

As you abide in Christ, His desires take precedence over yours. The more you abide, the more you will see this fully and begin to desire the things of God. What you want becomes secondary to what God wants for you. As you abide in Him, your wants begin to mirror His.

So often we invite God to become a part of *our* plan. And we feel generous and spiritual for doing so. This is completely backward. Many times in our lives we have prayed, "Lord, You know I'm going to start doing such and so tomorrow. I ask You to be a part of it." What we needed to do was ask God whether He even wanted us involved in the project. As you begin abiding, you'll stop making plans of your own, hoping or expecting Him to join you in them. Through prayer, you'll go directly to Him and seek His plans for your life.

Prayer is simply talking to God. You might begin to pray something like this:

> *Lord, I often forget that You are with me, in me. Help me today to develop this as a habit. Amen.*

As your day unfolds, send up frequent prayers to the Lord. These might be something such as:

> *Lord, You are with me; You live within me. The children will be home soon, please give me all that I need to tenderly welcome them. Lord, I am working. I have deadlines to meet. I feel stress with a coworker. I ask for Your wisdom. Lord, my husband seems removed and quiet. Please love him through me. Help me reach out and comfort him. Lord, I am in a situation where gossip abounds. Help me not to contribute to this. Help me to guard*

the reputation of my husband. Help me to turn this conversation to another path.

As you send "arrow" prayers to the Lord throughout the day, your mind will be renewed, as will your heart and your strength. These prayers, however, cannot take the place of a concentrated prayer time with God. As you pray, you will gain a new perspective—an eternal perspective—and feel the presence of the Lord filling you as you commit your day and all that unfolds to Him.

BEGINNING YOUR DAY

How do you begin your day? Do you stay in bed until the last second and then rush to get yourself and your family ready?

Try beginning the day with prayer. Make a decision today to make quiet time with the Lord a priority as you begin your day. We do some practical things to help us have "blanket victory"—victory over blankets and a cozy bed!

1. Ask the Lord to awaken you Himself. It is amazing how often you will suddenly find yourself wide-awake at your requested time.
2. Make coffee the night before, using an automatic timer. When you begin your prayer time, the coffee is freshly made and ready for you. If you're not a coffee drinker, you might enjoy a steaming cup of hot tea, which takes just seconds to make.
3. If you need an alarm, put it out of reach, perhaps on your dresser or outside your door. This way you'll have taken the first five steps out of bed, which are the most difficult, and you'll have obtained forward momentum.

4. Consider getting up fifteen to twenty minutes before your family. This will ease you gently into your morning and allow you a few minutes of time with the Lord before beginning your day.

5. Begin prayer on your knees if it is physically possible for you. We find that this position reminds us of the holiness of God. It also quickens us as to our need for Him and helps us acknowledge that we are surrendered to Him.

6. Keep your Bible and devotionals in a basket or box next to your prayer spot. This will prevent a frantic search for them in the morning.

7. Faithfully read God's Word and be obedient to it. Jesus said: "If anyone loves me, he will obey my teaching. My Father will love him, and we will come to him and make our home with him" (John 14:23).

8. Consider journaling. Write a few sentences in a notebook. Our journal entries vary. Sometimes we write purely to praise God or to thank Him. Other times it is about a problem we are facing. Our writing style is simple and conversational. We both have a place in our journals where we keep written prayer requests for family, friends, those in Christian service, our own ministries, and worldwide needs. Highlight His answers to prayer with a colored marker. Soon you will see your own journal peppered with color!

If you are unaccustomed to a regular prayer time, you might be wondering how to begin. Many people divide their prayer time using the acrostic ACTS.

A — Adore God; acknowledge who He is
(Hebrews 13:15).

C — Confess your sins (1 John 1:9).

T — Thank Him for what He has done in your life
(1 Thessalonians 5:18).

S — Supplication: Pray for yourself and others
(James: 5:16).

You may want to read a passage of Scripture. Devotionals are also helpful in giving direction for this time. We've listed three devotionals we recommend:

1. *Daily Light Devotional* by Anne Graham Lotz (J. Countryman).
2. *31 Days of Praise* by Ruth and Warren Myers (Multnomah Publishers, Inc.).
3. *31 Days of Prayer* by Ruth and Warren Myers (Multnomah Publishers, Inc.).

There are a number of other devotionals that you might enjoy. Ask your pastor and friends what they use. Visit your local Christian bookstore. Regardless of what you find, though, don't let anything take the place of your prayer time with God or reading from His Word.

PRACTICE

It takes approximately three weeks to form a habit. If you want to be increasingly aware that Jesus is in you and that you are in Him, put reminders of this around your home and office. Set a timer to go off every hour for a few days, and when it does, thank Him for His presence and for what He's doing in your life. Put Post-it notes on your makeup mirror or your refrigerator door. Your heart will overflow with love as you increasingly train your mind to be on Him.

Sadly, one can slip out of abiding in Christ. A common cause is allowing hurt feelings to rule behavior.

Abiding in Christ is a powerful thing. As you abide, you will find yourself responding to your husband and others differently. Frequently their responses will also change as they witness the Holy Spirit at work in your life.

Sadly, one can slip out of abiding with Christ. Several things can cause this: disobedience, pride, and unforgivingness, to mention a few. Another common cause is allowing hurt feelings to rule behavior.

PAINTING AND ABIDING

It was late October, and my (Connie) husband and I were trying to finish painting our home before winter set in. As the afternoon wound down, dark clouds appeared overhead. A rainstorm appeared imminent, but we decided that if we hurried, we could get the garage painted before the storm hit.

We painted as quickly as we could, racing against the clouds. Just as we finished the last board, large raindrops began to fall. The paint was water-based and hadn't dried. As the rain fell, the fresh paint began to run. Within minutes, the entire area was streaked and looked far worse than it did originally. Not only that, but the old paint had begun to peel anew and would have to be prepped again—a long, arduous task.

The rains were short-lived and the sun reappeared, quickly drying the wet wood. My husband worked for over an hour to get the area ready to be repainted. He then left for his evening shift at work.

He came home the next morning exhausted. After eating a quick bite of breakfast, he headed to our room to sleep. Early in the afternoon, a thought hit me. I would surprise him by repainting the ruined area.

Even though there were once again ominous looking clouds overhead, I began. *Surely it won't rain two afternoons in a row,* I said to myself. It was a foolish thought, for the clouds were darker than they'd been on the previous day.

Unbelievably, just as I was finishing, I felt a raindrop. In dismay I looked up into the sky just as the rain came pouring down. I quickly gathered up my supplies and headed indoors. Though disappointed, I knew my husband would be touched by my efforts.

A bit later, my husband awoke and came into the kitchen. I showed him how I had attempted to repaint the wall. The day was dark and gloomy and the rain continued falling as we talked.

"Was it cloudy like this when you began?" he asked.

"Yes," I said, laughing, "but I thought this time I could surely beat the rain."

"I wish you hadn't done that," he said in frustration. "Now I have to prep the wood for a third time. From now on, if there are rain clouds in the sky, *don't paint.*"

It seemed to me that my husband was doing far more scolding than he was commending. I was expecting him to be moved by my actions, and he was! But not in the way I had expected.

My feelings were hurt. I couldn't understand his response. Although at the time I wasn't consciously thinking of doing this, I decided to bear a grudge against him for the rest of the evening. I was cool and aloof. Later that night, he again left for his job. There was an uneasiness in my spirit as there always is when I cease abiding and allow hurt feelings to dictate my behavior. I tried to dismiss it and went to bed.

Early the next morning, I got out of bed for my quiet time with the Lord. The restlessness was still there. I asked Jesus to reveal to me anything I needed to correct in regard to the paint issue. Instantly, I felt convicted that my grudge bearing and cool attitude had been wrong and that my pride needed to be replaced with humility.

"Humility, Lord?" I asked. "Why are You pressing me to be humble when *he* is at fault?" I might as well have been in the Garden with Eve, for I was trying to blame someone else for my sin.

As I sat at His feet and talked with Him, I realized that as long as I called myself His, I was called to be humble. It is the very essence of who He is, and it should be the same for me. How easy it is to push this aside when pride and hurt feelings kick in.

As I prayed, the Lord gave me a glimpse into my own heart. What a mess it was. It is easy to let yourself off the hook if you are constantly looking for the wrong in others. I was grieved at my behavior. I asked the Lord's forgiveness and knew I needed to do the same of my husband. About that time the back door opened. My husband, remembering my mood from the previous evening, briefly acknowledged me and headed to our room to sleep.

"Wait!" I said. "I need to say something." He came back and sat down in the chair beside me.

"I'm so sorry I was cold toward you last night. I was wrong. Will you forgive me?"

His spirit softened instantly. "I was wrong too," he said, "but when I looked out at the wet paint, all I could see was the time it would take to prep it again. Plus I was tired from working nights. I'm sorry."

His entire body seemed to relax then. He leaned back in the chair and began talking about his previous night at work. He works in a busy hospital, and during his shift a couple had come in holding their nonresponsive baby in their arms. Though the medical staff did all it could, the baby couldn't be revived. My husband talked about how sad the parents were, and his eyes misted as he spoke of our own children sleeping peacefully just a few rooms away. He shared how inadequate he felt trying to comfort the grieving parents.

He went on to speak of a second case in which a young man had tried to commit suicide. The man said he felt helpless, hopeless, and had no reason to live. My husband sat and talked with him and told him about Someone who gives hope. The man repented of his sins and trusted Jesus to be his Savior. As my husband told me this news, his eyes lit up and a smile crossed his face. He then went to get some rest.

Had I not sought the Lord, I feel sure I wouldn't have apologized so quickly, if at all. I would have continued to hold on to my hurt. My husband would have gone straight to bed, and a wonderful sharing opportunity would have been lost.

This is just one example of what can happen as you abide in Christ. He equips you to bear fruit. Apart from Him, you can do *nothing*.

Familiarize yourself with the red flags that indicate you are no longer abiding. These might include a critical spirit, thoughts of revenge, indifference, cold treatment toward another, unforgiving-ness, grudge bearing, and primarily, no longer spending time with God—or doing so in a rushed, "have-to" manner.

In a letter to believers in Galatia, Paul said, "You were running a good race. Who cut in on you and kept you from obeying the truth? That kind of persuasion *does not* come from the one who calls you" (Galatians 5:7–8). Purpose to abide in the One who called you. Should you discover that you are no longer abiding, run to Him! Ask Him to help you begin abiding again.

ABIDING IS FOUNDATIONAL

Women often want their marriages to change, but they have no idea that this has anything to do with abiding. It has everything to do with abiding! *Abiding is foundational to getting what you want.*

Many think of marriage as one compartment of their lives and abiding as another. They separate the two. They feel compelled to work on the barriers in their marriage, yet never consider this prin-ciple of abiding. What they don't realize is that the two cannot be separated.

Everything in your life is affected when you abide! When you are truly at home in Christ, it will transcend all that you do. Regardless of the trials you are currently facing, the first step is to abide in Christ, drawing on His strength and wisdom.

Will your marriage improve if you abide? You can't predict this because another person's choices are involved. However, every aspect of *your* life will be colored by your choosing to abide. We encourage you to abide continually in Christ, not only as you endeavor to strengthen your marriage, but in your everyday life as well.

NOT SOMEHOW, BUT TRIUMPHANTLY

Every four years when the Olympics come around, we enjoy watching women's gymnastics. The balance beam is considered by most to be the toughest of the four apparatuses. The competitors perform all sorts of jumps, turns, and whirls on the narrow board, but the overriding goal is to *stay on the beam.* Many will get off balance just a tiny bit, and you can see them fighting to stay atop the beam, using every available muscle to keep from falling.

Abiding is similar to this. You want to abide—stay atop the beam—*regardless!* You may stumble and trip, and life may throw some real challenges your way, but no matter what, *stay on the beam!* Don't allow anything—pride, anger, rejection, hurt, unforgivingness—to cause you to fall. If you do, get up quickly and *get back on the beam!*

A. Wetherell Johnson, a woman whose love for the Lord has impacted thousands of lives, believed that through abiding in Christ, you can live "not somehow, but triumphantly."[7]

Don't those words have a beautiful ring? You can do it through abiding. The "somehow" of your life will slowly give way to "triumphant" as you hand the worn and tattered oars over to the One who powers the boat.

Aren't you tired of rowing? There's no reason to row any longer. A stronger set of arms is waiting to hold you, enfold you, and direct the course of your life from this point forward.

"Not somehow, but triumphantly!" May this be your heart's desire as you seek to abide in Him.

"Not somehow, but triumphantly!" May you settle for nothing less.

Part Three

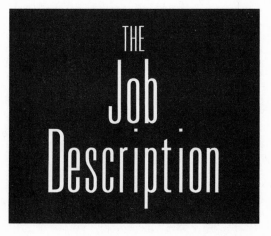

THE
Job
Description

Chapter Five: Who's in Charge Around Here Anyway?

Submission in marriage. If you want to heat up a conversation, simply mention those words. We attended a large gathering recently, and this topic was mentioned. Various things were being discussed all around us, but once these words were spoken, they spread like wildfire through the room. Within seconds, most everyone was debating someone else on the topic. People jockeyed to get the floor, and no sooner would someone begin to speak than someone else would interrupt or correct. Until this time, the mood of the party had been pleasant and understated, but now emotion ran rampant. "I'd say someone hit a nerve," a friend mused wryly. "A *raw* nerve."

A raw nerve indeed. In writing this book, we spoke with dozens of women on a number of subjects. Yet none generated the controversy that submission did. Many chafed at the mere mention of the word. Said one woman, "I can barely stand to hear 'that word' spoken aloud." We found this to be a common reaction among Christian and non-Christian women alike. Wary and cautious, today's woman is uncertain whether submission any longer fits into her lifestyle. In this chapter, we hope to clearly delineate what God says about this issue and exhort you to consider whether your stand lines up with God's plan!

Submission in marriage—God's design for your best.

Who's in Charge Around Here Anyway?

It is no small thing when a woman
chooses God's way over her own.

He was the last one off of the plane. When his wife, holding their younger daughter, saw him, she ran to his open arms. They were oblivious to the people waiting to board. Their embrace was deeply touching and prolonged.

Lingering behind was their older daughter, about six years of age. As soon as Dad could let go of Mom, he knelt and swept her into a bear hug. They were lost in their own world.

Then Dad began to reach for the small daughter still in her mother's arms—but she wouldn't go to him. Mom kept turning this way and that so he could see her, but she was covering her eyes with her hands. She didn't remember him! He respected her unwillingness with a loving pat.

As they walked past me (Nancy), I heard the older child confide, "Oh, Daddy! You were gone so long and we missed you so much!" It was then that I read the word printed in capital letters on the back of his jacket: NAVY.

It brought back memories of this same scenario when my father was in the Air Force years ago. I was seven years old and the older sister. I hadn't seen him for almost two years. My younger sister, born shortly after Dad's departure, had never laid eyes on him.

What could keep men who obviously adored their families away from their loved ones for months, even years? Like the stranger in the airport and my own beloved father, when you serve your country in the military, you submit to those in authority over you. If this were not so, our country would become unprotected quickly. We would eventually be taken over by a country whose soldiers *were* compliant. At the very core of our freedom is the principle of *submission to authority.*

A PRINCIPLE IN EVERYDAY LIFE

Perhaps you've never thought about it, but this principle is at work all around you in everyday life. It is the way governments and businesses are run, and it's necessary for maintaining order.

Suppose you went to a fast-food restaurant and everyone wanted to work the counters, but no one was willing to prepare the food. What would it be like if you went to the grocery store and because all the employees wanted to be assigned to the bakery that day, no one stocked the shelves or checked your items at the register? Schools would close if all teachers decided that being a physical education instructor was more fun than teaching English or math. The children might become trained athletes, but they would never learn to read or write.

Can you imagine what life would be like without this underlying principle of authority? It would be chaotic, nonfunctional, and, in some cases, life threatening. In the military, this authority is outlined in governmental operating procedures. In the business world, it is delineated by corporate guidelines. In the home, it is declared by the Word of God.

DECLARED BY THE WORD OF GOD

When you get married, another of your wedding gifts from God is an umbrella He gives you for protection. It has a name: submission. How do we know this was given by God? Because He tells us so in His word:

> Wives, submit to your husbands as to the Lord. (Ephesians 5:22)

This principle in marriage is often skipped, laughed at, or scorned. It is ignored and derided much to the detriment of the woman it was meant to bless. To most women, there is no flag so red as the flag of submission.

Submission Defined

Just what does submission mean? If you ask a dozen people, chances are you'll get a dozen answers. Here is a simple definition:

Submission is *voluntarily cooperating with another out of love and respect for God and for that person.*[1]

Perhaps this definition will change your view of submission, as it did for one woman. She said, "Hey, I can do that...I want to do that. I don't want not to do that!" Double negative aside, this woman caught a glimmer of God's best for her and said, "I can do it." She said later that her previous failures had occurred because she left God out of the equation.

Have you done this too? If you have, no wonder you're struggling! Leaving God out of the equation is like going deep-sea diving without an oxygen tank. You'd be so busy bobbing to the top for air that you'd never discover the treasures on the ocean floor.

Did you notice that the definition of submission didn't include the words *inferior to* or *less than?* Frequently, these words are interwoven with our idea of what submission means. But this is wrong thinking! A wife isn't inferior to her husband in any way. We are told in Genesis that they are created equal in God's image (1:27). This is reiterated in the New Testament: "There is [now no distinction]…there is not male and female; for you are all one in Christ Jesus" (Galatians 3:28, AMP).

Submission is not an issue of superiority.

The Chain of Authority

Submission is not an issue of superiority. There is no differentiation in the body of Christ as far as spiritual privilege and position are concerned. However, Paul clearly states that there is headship of the man over the woman.

> Now I want you to realize that the head of every man is Christ, and the head of the woman is man, and the head of Christ is God. (1 Corinthians 11:3)

We are under our husbands' authority—and ultimately God's. Submission is not a demeaning thing.

This is a hard concept for most people to grasp. We're equal to our husbands, yet we're still under their authority. Being under someone simply means that you have less authority than they do—not that you're worth less. This in itself is a problem for many women because we like being the authorities, don't we? Or at least the coauthorities. Yet God, in His infinite wisdom, decided to place woman not under every man's authority but under her husband's authority.

Paul goes on to say, "Neither was man created for woman, but woman for man" (v. 9). This is also a difficult thing for many women to swallow. But this is God's plan. As we said in chapter 1, God didn't consider creation complete until He created woman. In no way was she looked upon as second-rate or as an afterthought. Her very existence helped define Adam.

God's intention is not to make you miserable, and He didn't send Jesus to the cross to assure you second-class citizenship. His death assured your *royal citizenship,* a citizenship in heaven (Philippians 3:20). This same love says, "Wives, submit to your husbands."

In the Home

There is a God-given chain of authority in the home. The husband is under the authority of God, and the wife is under her husband's authority. In a sense, your husband is the president and you are the vice president. Do you find at times that rather than concentrating on the vice presidency, you are eyeing the office of president? Or maybe you have already made a successful takeover bid and appointed yourself to his position.

Imagine that you've just been asked to interview for the job of vice president in a Fortune 500 company. It is a prestigious position, and you will be reporting directly to the president, the owner's son. You go in for the interview and a copy of the job description is given to you to review. Do you ask to see a copy of the president's job description? Of course not! That is none of your concern. Your concern is your own job description. Do you go into the job thinking that you will take the presidency away from the president? No, you concentrate on your own job. You have no authority to fire the president. This power lies with someone much higher than you.

This example holds true in your marriage as well. What you are to concentrate on is your own job description. You are responsible for your role. Your husband is responsible for his. What if you do your job, but he doesn't do his? That is between him and the Father. God will deal with a disobedient or ungodly husband. Your concern is whether or not you're doing your job well, and you can gauge this by your obedience.

Submission Requires Strength

Ten years ago, my family and I (Connie) lived by Puget Sound in Tacoma, Washington. One summer day, our neighbors called and said they were going to hike a nearby trail. It was supposed to be an especially beautiful trail, and we agreed to go with them. After packing a picnic lunch, we headed out. We drove to the bottom of the trail, got out of our cars, and began the hike. The spot to which we had driven was already high up in the mountains, and we would be climbing even farther. It was a gorgeous day. The air was cool and crisp, and the view was majestic. My husband and I took turns carrying our three-month-old daughter in her carrier, and our four-year-old twins scampered along the trail with the other children. As we marched along, we all agreed that this was a day we'd long remember.

After stopping for lunch, we set out again. Before long, we came to the mountain's edge. A suspension bridge loomed before us, connecting the mountain on which we were now standing to another mountain several hundred feet beyond. Below the bridge ran a large, thundering river. Due to the heavy spring rains, it flowed at a furious pace. Its waters hit the rocks with a mighty crash, and the turbulence was so great that we had to raise our voices to be heard. The water turned white as it tumbled over and over itself on its way downstream.

"Shall we go across?" my friend asked the rest of the group. "Or are you ready to go back?"

What a silly question to ask six children and two adventuresome men!

"Go across!" they shouted enthusiastically.

"Go back!" I said. "There's no way I'm going to cross that bridge. It's already swaying all over the place. What do you think will happen when all of us get on it? It could break!"

I am not a water person. I am comfortable in a bathtub, but beyond that I become nervous. I didn't learn to swim until I took a beginning course in college, and even then I spent most of the time at the bottom of the pool. The thought of crossing that long, wobbly bridge, which appeared to me to be hanging perilously, seemed insane.

"Come on, honey. I'll help you across," my husband offered.

"I'll get on your other side and help," our neighbor said. "We'll go as slowly as you want."

"No, I'll just sit here with the baby and wait until you come back," I said. "You go ahead. I don't mind a bit."

But they wouldn't hear of it. It was all or none. I took a deep breath. "Okay, I'll cross." Then I turned to my husband and warned, "Don't you dare pretend to throw me overboard." My husband threw back his head in laughter and agreed.

With one final look at the mountain upon which my feet firmly rested, off we went. The other adults interspersed themselves among the children, and I brought up the rear. They crossed quickly, while I literally inched my way along. I'm sure I looked a bit idiotic going so slowly, but I didn't care. With every grip of the rope, I braced myself for the bridge to give way. After getting our girls safely across, my husband ran back to help me. I was practically on my hands and knees as I stepped off of the bridge. Everyone cheered wildly! I felt as though I had just won a gold medal in the decathlon! We set off on the second leg of the trip, and it was even more beautiful than the first. Had I been unwilling to cross the bridge, I would never have experienced what lay beyond.

Submission in marriage is similar. The first mountain represents those women who refuse, for whatever reason, to submit to their husbands. Guided by their feelings and the mentality of modern times, they feel secure in their footing and see no reason to change.

The other mountain represents those women who have chosen to be submissive. Their lives are characterized by an overriding sense of peace, even when the storm clouds rumble overhead. This is a rare thing. The only way to get from the first mountain to the second is over a bridge called obedience.

Do you feel that only weak women cross this bridge? That

couldn't be further from the truth. Submission is not for the weak-willed or fainthearted. It requires true discipline and supernatural strength.

This could well be one of the most exciting and liberating principles you will ever discover! Regardless of whether your marriage changes or not, you will be changed, and it will bring about a closer walk with God. God blesses obedience.

Submission is not for the weak-willed or fainthearted. It requires true discipline and supernatural strength.

YOUR OPINION COUNTS

Does this mean a wife cannot appeal her husband's decisions? Definitely not! In my own marriage (Nancy), if I want to do something—visit my father, for example—and Ray doesn't want me to go at that time, I appeal to him, presenting my reasons. And in the end I do what he asks.

This happened several years ago. I had just come home from a three-day retreat, walked in the door, and greeted Ray when the phone rang. It was my beloved dad, who wanted me to come to his home in Virginia to care for him after elective surgery. I thought surely Ray would agree, but he didn't. I expressed my surprise at his decision and my strong desire to go. He explained that he didn't mind if I went the following week, but that since I had just returned home he wanted to be with me. After all, he reasoned, it was elective and not emergency surgery. So I stayed home. This was very difficult, and I was not happy about it, but I privately forgave him. My sister did go, however. She told me later that it meant the world to her and that she and Dad had bonded in a way they had not before—and Dad was eighty-nine and she was fifty-five! Dad passed away in September. Christine and I were both at his bedside, deeply connected to him and each other—with no regrets.

THE HUSBAND'S LEADERSHIP

How can you get your husband to be the leader in your home? Simply put, you can't. *He already is the leader.* God made that clear in the Garden. But you can help your husband assume the leadership role. You do this by introducing into your marriage the things God tells you to do in His Word. When you do, the results can be far-reaching.

Although he has the authority to do so, the husband doesn't necessarily make all the decisions. A wise man sees his wife's giftedness in certain areas and delegates those responsibilities to her. But if the husband wants things one way and the wife another, the husband is to make the final decision. What if he's dead wrong, as can be the case? This is often the way he learns to consider more carefully his wife's opinion in the future. If she insists on her own way, however, she sows contentiousness and reaps bitterness and division.

One of the privileges of submission is that a woman no longer takes the consequences of a decision upon herself. When she submits to her husband and allows him to lead, the consequences fall on him.

SUBMISSION'S FRUIT

Submitting to our husbands out of obedience to God's Word is all the motive we need, yet Peter tells us that there may be another result as well: "So that, if any of them do not believe the word, they may be won over without words by the behavior of their wives" (1 Peter 3:1).

Your godly behavior may be used by God to influence your husband for eternal good, whether that means winning him to the Savior or influencing his walk with God. It may happen in a matter of weeks, or it may take years.

A Husband Who Was Won to the Word

In his book *Straight Talk*, James Dobson, president and founder of Focus on the Family ministries, gives a beautiful example of this. He talks about his paternal grandfather, R. L. Dobson. R. L. Dobson was a good and moral man, but saw no need for the Christian faith.

This spiritual disinterest placed his grandmother under great pressure. She was a devout Christian who felt she must put God first. Therefore, she accepted the responsibility of introducing her six children to Jesus Christ. In Dr. Dobson's words:

> There were times when my grandfather placed tremendous pressure on my grandmother—not to give up her faith, but to leave him out of it.
>
> He said, "I am a good father and provider, I pay my bills, and I am honest in dealing with my fellow man. That is enough."
>
> His wife replied, "You are a good man, but that is not enough. You should give your heart to God." This he could not comprehend.
>
> My ninety-seven-pound grandmother made no attempt to force her faith on her husband, nor did she treat him disrespectfully. But she quietly continued to pray and

fast for the man she loved. For more than forty years she brought this same petition before God on her knees.

Then, at sixty-nine years of age, my grandfather suffered a stroke, and for the first time in his life he was desperately ill. One day his young daughter came into his room to clean and straighten. As she walked by his bed, she saw tears in his eyes. No one had ever seen him cry before.

"Daddy, what's wrong?" she asked.

He responded, "Honey, go to the head of the stairs and call your mother."

My grandmother ran to her husband's side and heard him say, "I know I'm going to die and I'm not afraid of death, but it's so dark. There's no way out. I've lived my whole life through and missed the one thing that really matters. Will you pray for me?"

"Will I pray?" exclaimed my grandmother. She had been hoping for that request throughout her adult life. She fell to her knees and the intercessions of forty years seemed to pour out through that bedside prayer. R. L. Dobson gave his heart to God that day in a wonderful way.

During the next two weeks, he asked to see some of the church people whom he had offended and requested their forgiveness. He concluded his personal affairs and then died with a testimony on his lips. Before descending into a coma from which he would never awaken, my grandfather said, "...Now there is a way through the darkness."

The unrelenting prayers of my little grandmother had been answered.[2]

HOW'S YOUR WALK?

There's a well-known saying that goes something like this:

> *Your talk talks,*
> *And your walk talks,*
> *But your walk talks*
> *More than your talk talks.*

That is what being "won over without words by the behavior of their wives" means. Our husbands are far more likely to respond to Christ if they see something in our lives that draws them to Him who lives in us, as Dr. Dobson's grandfather saw in his grandmother. Had she been a wife who nagged, cajoled, pleaded, and scolded, *why would her husband want what she had?* Your actions speak far louder than what you say. The results are in God's hands.

SUBMISSION EXEMPLIFIED

What we believe is expressed in the way we behave.

The way we behave reveals our character.

Our character is determined by the choices we make.

Those choices begin with a decision made in our minds.

And these decisions are activated by our wills.

This is what God sees. "God sees not as man sees, for man looks at the outward appearance, but the LORD looks at the heart" (1 Samuel 16:7, NASB).

We've chosen six qualities of godly women, along with the opposite traits. The opposite traits closely parallel the excuses many women make regarding their lack of submission in marriage.

1. Humility Versus Pride

Love is not proud. (1 Corinthians 13:4)

Many women lack a willingness to follow God's directive in the area of humility. As they read their Bibles, women see for themselves what it has to say on the matter of submission and discuss it at length. Yet many still disregard the principle of submission. Often it is not a lack of understanding that keeps them from submitting, but a proud heart. Many women, after reading a passage, ask, "Why should I? Until he changes, why should I?" Their reasons seem genuine, but underneath lurks pride. Frequently a woman filled with pride is stubborn and contentious in her marriage.

Your choice to obey God must take precedence over your rationalization for taking over the leadership role in your home.

Ultimately, when you say, "I'm doing my part but he's not doing his," you are boasting. You can make yourself look awfully good when you weigh your efforts against your husband's. But this doesn't change what the Lord has asked of you.

When your child comes to you to tattle on a sibling, do you ever say, "You don't need to worry about that"? The same lesson applies here. It is freeing to realize that we don't have to keep score.

Other common justifications for taking over your husband's role include:

- "He's not as smart, sensitive, or mature as I am."
- "He's not a believer, or as good a Christian, or as biblically literate as I am."

- "The Lord has gifted me with a discerning spirit, so I'll make the better decision."
- "Leadership is not his forte, but it is mine. Therefore he cannot lead, but I can. I am leading our family because he isn't (or can't, or won't, or does it wrong). I have no other choice."

Your choice here is to obey God, and this must take precedence over your rationalization for taking over the leadership role in your home. There is no way you can do both. A woman may feel that her husband actually wants her to lead. Could it be that because his leading never suited her, it simply became easier to allow her to lead than to be criticized constantly? The bottom line is this:

> God has called your husband to lead.
> He has called you
> to help your husband succeed
> in that role.
> Any attempt on your part
> to wrestle the leadership role
> from your husband
> is sin.

There is no way around this truth, even if your husband is a nonbeliever. He is still to be the leader of your home. In other words, your submission isn't about your husband's behavior. It's about your own. Don't try to convince yourself otherwise.

If pride is your sin, humbly confess this sin to God. When you humble yourself in the presence of God, He will exalt you (James 4:10)!

2. Trust Versus Fearfulness

Love...trusts God always. (1 Corinthians 13:7, *The Message*)

It was an awakening for me (Connie) when I realized that submission was really a trust issue: Could I trust God enough to obey His command? Once I understood this, the issue for me was no longer about submitting; it was about trusting God. I was reminded of my dad swimming in the deep end of a swimming pool. He would often say to my youngest sister, who was standing on the deck, "Jump in and I'll catch you." My sister, who couldn't swim, would jump into his arms every time because she trusted him. This example pales in comparison to how greatly we can trust Jesus Christ.

3. Selflessness Versus Self-Centeredness

Love cares more for others than for self. (1 Corinthians 13:4, *The Message*)

Ephesians 5:21 says that we are to submit to one another out of reverence for Christ, but the very next verse specifically instructs women to submit themselves to their husbands as to the Lord. Yet many women are intent on running things their way. This is self-centeredness.

An article on February 21, 1998, in the *Omaha World-Herald* entitled "The Secret to a Happy Marriage? Men Giving In" says that if men want their marriages to last for a long time, the answer is simple: "Just do what your wife says. Go ahead, give in to her."

According to the article, John Gottman, of the University of Washington, studied 130 newlywed couples for six years in an effort to find ways to predict both marital success and failure. He and his colleagues discovered that those marriages that worked well had one thing in common—the husband was willing to give in to the wife.

This is in direct opposition to the Word of God! When you were a little girl, did you ever have a friend come over to play? Surely one of your friends was bossy. You had to do what she wanted or else she'd go home! Remember how that made you feel? Is that how your husband feels?

Submitting to your husband displays not only your love for him, but your love for God as well. It is foundational for being a helper to your husband.

4. Integrity Versus Manipulation

Love...doesn't force itself on others. (1 Corinthians 13:5, *The Message*)

Do you know how to get the leadership position in your home? Sure you do! We all do! Tears, silence, pouting, harboring grudges, withholding sex, snide remarks, tantrums, and guilt, to name a few. This is called manipulation and is the tool women use most often in holding onto or striving for the leadership role.

Manipulation means to control another by artful, unfair, or insidious means *for one's own advantage.* Proverbs 11:1 says that "the LORD *abhors* dishonest scales." Doesn't this inspire you to want to avoid manipulation and be a woman of integrity?

Are you a manipulative woman? Is a power struggle going on in your home? Are you playing tug-of-war with your husband about who will assume the leadership position? There was a time when that was true in my life (Nancy), and it didn't last for just a short period either. It was a twenty-three-year power struggle, and it occurred because I lacked wisdom.

5. Wisdom Versus Ignorance

Love…takes pleasure in the flowering of truth.
(1 Corinthians 13:6, *The Message*)

In my ignorance, I (Nancy) didn't understand fully what was happening. I was married for twenty-one years before I owned a Bible. I didn't know what God expected of me as a wife. After receiving Christ as my Savior in 1981 and learning God's principles for marriage, I was shocked. I had thought I was nearly perfect. How arrogant I was. *If only my husband would change,* I thought, *I'd be so happy.* But the more I got into God's Word, the more convicted I became. *I need to change, Lord, and by Your grace I will.*

I realized I had been self-centered, manipulative, and unforgiving. I pored over the marriage verses in Scripture, and one by one, without announcing what I was doing, incorporated them into my life. In the beginning, when I was still immature, I didn't think my husband deserved this. Isn't that an awful way to start? But I wanted to please God, so I began. Will *you?*

6. Surrender Versus Control

Love does not demand its own way. (1 Corinthians 13:5, TLB)

Maybe you are like the woman who told her friend, "I want to obey Christ, but no matter how hard I try, submission just isn't my spiritual gift." Submission is not a spiritual gift. It is a choice! As one woman told us, "My husband insists that when I say I want him to be the leader in our home, what I really want is to hear my words coming out of his mouth."

Does this define your attitude toward leadership in the home?

Ultimately the whole subject of submission boils down to one issue—control. Letting go of control in the home is a difficult thing for most women. Until you're willing to let go of this, you're missing out on God's plan for your life.

Manipulation is the tool women use most often in holding onto or striving for the leadership role.

I (Connie) have a wonderful friend named Sandy who is the busy mother of five boys. Just short of their twenty-fifth anniversary, Sandy's husband, Mike, was near death after a three-month struggle with cancer. The night before he died, a small group of friends gathered with Sandy at his bedside. We sang, prayed, read Scripture, and reminisced. Sandy shared a story that most of us had never heard. She told how several years earlier, their family had gone to Mexico to share the gospel. They had a great love for the Mexican people and went there annually. Their boys, which included two sets of twins, were seven and younger at the time.

They had been in Mexico for several days and were scheduled to leave the following day. Sandy was feeling sick, as were some of the boys, and she was more than ready to get back to the comforts of home. Their plans were to take a bus out the following evening.

"Can't we leave earlier in the day and not wait until evening?" Sandy asked Mike.

"No," Mike said. "I don't think we should leave before evening."

Sandy asked again, but Mike remained insistent, saying, "I feel strongly that we should leave in the evening."

"Okay, you're in charge. I'll go along with your wishes."

As she told us later, "I had lived my life trying to be a submissive wife, so I felt the final decision was up to him.

"We got on the bus about seven that night. We drove all night, and at about four the next morning, the bus came to a sudden stop. The passengers woke up, alarmed. We were nowhere near our destination. The driver had gotten a brief radio message that there had been a bad accident and that we could go no farther. He knew no details.

"It was only later that we found out that Hurricane Gilberto had wreaked havoc farther up the road we were traveling. A main bridge had been hit and had disappeared into the river below. The morning bus, which I wanted to take so badly, was en route and received no warning of the impending danger. The driver had no time to react as the bus topped the hill. It plunged into the roaring river below. Everyone on the bus died. Five policemen were killed trying to save some of the people. Had I insisted that we leave earlier, our lives would have been lost as well. My own. My husband's. Our five boys'. I feel the Lord used Mike to spare us."

"He used you too," we told her. "You could have insisted on leaving. You were sick, as were the boys. Undoubtedly, you could have worn Mike down and convinced him to leave earlier. But you didn't, because you wanted to submit to his leadership."

Perhaps you're thinking, *But what if it had been the other way around, and the evening bus had crashed instead?* The result would seem tragic. We asked Sandy this very thing, and her response was, "Well, then we would have been in heaven with Jesus. I feel I would have done the right thing even then. We can't always understand the circumstances, but we can always trust Him."

It is impossible to analyze every angle of every situation before deciding to submit to one's husband. What is possible, though, is to obey God's Word and trust Him for the outcome.

"I'LL DO MY PART WHEN..."

As we've talked to women over the past few years, we've found that the most common excuse for not carrying out God's role in their marriages is, "I'll do my part when he does his." At the root of this statement lies disobedience.

Whether your husband is doing his part or not has absolutely nothing to do with your obedience to God. Perhaps you hold to the verse in Ephesians 5:21 that says we're to submit to one another out of reverence for Christ. Ideally this is true—a Spirit-filled person would be sensitive to others' needs and willingly serve them. There would be no domination or self-promotion. This is true for both men and women, but the husband's headship, as determined by God in the Garden, remains intact regardless of whether he chooses this behavior or not.

This verse, however, in no way negates the following verse: "Wives, submit to your husbands as to the Lord" (v. 22). The latter doesn't depend on the former as many would like to think. Wives are directed specifically to submit even though their husbands may not treat them in the same considerate manner. A husband's failure to obey verse 21 doesn't excuse or justify a wife's disobedience of verse 22. (Note: There are moral limits to submission; it is only *as is fitting in the Lord.* A wife is not obligated to follow her husband's leadership if it conflicts with specific scriptural commands.[3] See "Exceptions" in the latter part of this chapter.)

Not to obey what you know to be God's command is

disobedience. It is willful rebellion—the very thing that was so costly to Eve. The only way to successfully submit, and bring glory to Christ as you do, is for your motive to be personal obedience to God's Word. There is no getting around this. Your success is determined by your desire to obey Christ.

A FINAL CAUTION

One last caution: Don't be tempted to use submission to veil what in reality is a cunning, resistant heart. To do so is deceitful. For example, let's say your husband is interviewing for a job in another town. You are happy where you are and don't want to leave the comfortable lifestyle you've carved out for yourself and your family. Perhaps the job is a promotion for your husband, or maybe it would simply cut his commute time in half. You have no intention of moving, but you know it should appear as if the decision is his. So when he asks you what you think, you assure him that you will do whatever he decides.

Don't throw up a sham of being submissive when you know in your heart that you're not.

In the meantime, though, you mention frequently how happy the children are at youth group and how the transition could be difficult for them. You throw in the names of friends whose children refuse to go to youth group to drive home your point. The next day, you say how much you appreciate your local school system and what a wonderful thing it is that your children have found their niches—especially Susie, who struggled so hard to find hers. You go on to mention that you don't know how she'll adapt to a new school, but probably she'll be okay. If you're lucky. At another time, you wonder aloud who will provide the Christian influence in your neighborhood if your husband takes the new job.

Do you see what's happening? In the end, your husband may think he made the decision, but you know better. It's perfectly legitimate to discuss worries and concerns, but discuss them outright and without ulterior motives. Don't throw up a sham of being submissive when you know in your heart that you're not. It can be tempting to do this, yet regardless of who else may be fooled, the Lord is not.

We can sometimes become shortsighted and lose perspective. We forget that life isn't just about the here and now, and often we strive to get our way in the smallest of matters. In reality, *all that really matters* is our obedience to God.

Think again about how obedience brings glory and honor to Jesus. Become awed all over again that you have something to offer Him. Think as well about how you want to be used by God. You don't want anything to hinder this. Our passion is to be used mightily for His kingdom. What a privilege! Yet we can prevent His using us when we disobey. We want the door to be wide open— not just mostly open or open most of the time.

SEVEN SIMPLE TIPS

Many times what is pleasing to God is seen as foolishness by the world. Certainly this is the case with submission. Here are seven simple tips that will help you go against the flow:

1. Ask the Lord to give your husband wisdom and discernment.
2. Raise the level of your expectations of God's power working in your husband's life. Have you put a limit on your expectations of what God can do?
3. Make a conscious effort to listen to your husband's point of view without quickly rejecting it.
4. Ask your children to seek their father's permission and counsel. My (Nancy) children initially asked, "Why? We haven't done this before." Even he questioned me because it was so far from the norm.
5. Affirm him when he makes a wise decision. Tell him how you saw the wisdom in what he did. Often a person rises to the level of another's trust in him.
6. Pray for your own obedience.
7. When you and your husband disagree on an issue, it is often a struggle to surrender your viewpoint. When his decisions prove to be wise, compliment him and express your confidence in his leadership. When he is wrong, as he sometimes will be, be gracious. Your attitude could well begin to build his respect for your wisdom.

EXCEPTIONS

You might be wondering whether there are exceptions in the area of submission. There are. God is the highest authority, and anything that goes against His Word should not be done. You are called first to submit to God's authority and then to your husband's. If submitting to your husband's authority violates God's teachings, then your choice must be to obey God, not your husband. Some of the exceptions are crystal clear: adultery, abuse, or asking you to worship other gods. There are many other areas that aren't as clear, and women wonder what to do in these cases. If you have such questions, or if your husband is asking you to do something illegal or immoral, you should take action. We suggest you:

- Seek counsel from God.
- Prayerfully appeal to your husband.
- Seek counsel from your pastor or other church leader you trust.

SUBMISSION IN THE GODHEAD

Submission is seen supremely in the Godhead: The head of Christ is God. Look again at 1 Corinthians 11:3:

> Now I want you to realize that the head of every man is Christ, and the head of the woman is man, and the head of Christ is God.

Jesus Himself, who is equal with His Father, submitted to His Father's will completely. In fact, He said, "My food is to do the will of Him who sent Me and to accomplish His work" (John 4:34, NASB). Regarding His will, He said, "I do not seek My own will, but the will of Him who sent Me" (John 5:30, NASB).

Isn't this the way you want to live your life? Is your food to do the will of God? Do you desire to accomplish His work? Then choose to submit all areas of your life to Him, as Jesus did, including submission to your husband.

Which do you think required more strength? To do His Father's will or to do His own? Was He weak or strong when He:

- gave up His glory to come to earth as a baby?
- gave up His voice, choosing to simply cry as a newborn?
- allowed Himself to be wrapped in swaddling clothes and cared for by Mary and Joseph?
- was subject to His earthly parents?
- was seized by human hands, mocked, spat upon, slapped, and scourged?
- went willingly to the cross, knowing the pain He would endure?
- refused the tauntings to come down from the cross and prove Himself God?
- endured the silence of His own Father when He became sin for the world?
- placed His own desires behind those of His Father?

Submission isn't a position of weakness, but strength. It is the key to a wholehearted commitment to God's Word and to becoming the wife God meant you to be.

Chapter Six: Behavior Matters

In 1986 one of the largest diamonds ever unearthed was found in the Premier Mine in Transvaal, South Africa. At 755.50 carats it displayed the color of a bright red rose at its core, changing to a golden yellow on the outer surfaces. Nothing like this had been seen before, and De Beers, the owner of the stone, turned to a master cutter for guidance. A team was assembled to cut the stone.

The preparations were amazing! An underground bunker was built so that there would be no vibrations as the gemologists worked. Great care was taken to see that the atmosphere was calm and peaceful. The walls were even painted a pale green to keep the eyes relaxed. The tools used were carefully made of dull metals so that the only shining object would be the stone itself. The entire process took three years, and when finished, the diamond weighed 545.67 carats. A group of businessmen from Thailand bought it as a gift for their king on the fiftieth anniversary of his reign.

Did you know that the Bible says there is something worth far more than jewels, something with which a 545-carat diamond cannot compare? It is a godly wife. She is precious in God's sight and of great value to Him. Are you a godly wife? Do you desire to become one? You can! Do you feel inept, unqualified, or just not up to it? God understands your feelings, your doubts, your fears. He also knows your heart and can work mightily in one that's yielded to Him. You are a diamond—a diamond in the rough, a diamond in the making. Place yourself into the hands of the Master Jeweler, Jesus Christ. Allow Him to chisel you, mold you, and refine you into the kind of wife that reflects His glory.

An excellent wife—she is worth far more than jewels!

Behavior Matters

Godly behavior is a jewel that
expresses the radiance of Christ.

"I've got a question for you," a seminar speaker recently announced to a large group of married women. "Raise your hand if you think it's important to be a good wife to your husband." Everyone in the group raised her hand. The speaker continued, "Now raise your hand if you consider yourself a good wife." Far fewer hands were raised. "How many of you feel you were a good wife at some point in your marriage but have gotten off track along the way?" The majority of women raised their hands. "My last question," the speaker said, "is how many of you would be willing to find out what God has to say about being a godly wife and then put those principles into practice?" Hand after hand after hand was raised. A sense of excitement and anticipation filled the room.

There was a similar scene recently as women met to discover just what it means to be a godly wife. Dozens of women came the first week. More came the second week as women brought their friends. And even more came the third week. The room was full and getting fuller. The word was out: Marriages could be changed. And the changes began when these women started to grasp what their God-given job descriptions were as wives.

Why do women feel it so important to be godly wives, yet so few feel that they are? For both of us, it was because we had no idea what our job description was as wives. Our focus in marriage had been wrong, as had been our motives for doing things.

In this chapter, you will begin to see what your job description is as a wife. A job is so much easier if you know what you're supposed to be doing! I (Connie) recently asked one of my daughters to clean the bathroom. She cleaned it and was finished in an amazingly short amount of time.

"Did you clean it thoroughly?" I asked.

"Yes," she said.

A while later I went in and looked it over. On the surface it appeared clean. But as I looked closer, I could see areas that hadn't been touched. I brought this to my daughter's attention.

"I didn't know to clean in those places, Mom. You've never really shown me how to clean the bathroom. You just tell me to clean it."

My daughter was right. She was doing the best job she could with the knowledge she had. I later taught her how to clean a bathroom thoroughly, and she's been doing so ever since.

That's often how it is for us in our roles as wives. We fall short because we don't know exactly what we're supposed to be doing. Hopefully after reading this chapter, your job description will be clearer and you will feel a renewed sense of purpose and joy in your role as a wife.

OBSERVABLE TRAITS

Peter spoke specifically of *purity* and *reverence* in marriage:

> ...when they observe the pure and modest way in which
> you conduct yourselves, together with your reverence. (1
> Peter 3:2, AMP)

We are going to examine these two observable traits. As we
express ways we've responded to our husbands, ask the Holy Spirit
to direct you in how to act and respond to your own husband.

Purity

Purity: to refrain from acts, thoughts, or desires that are not
sanctioned by the marriage vows. To be modest in deport-
ment and dress as the outward sign of inward purity.

As is evident in this definition, purity is something inward as
well as outward, involving our thoughts and actions.

Our Thoughts

We see from David's life that adultery begins in the thought life.
David saw Bathsheba bathing. He *thought* about her, sent for her,
conceived a child with her, and ordered her husband to the front
lines in battle, knowing he would be killed (2 Samuel 11). We see
that David, "a man after God's own heart," struggled with his
thought life, and it led to a very serious sin.

You can't always choose the thoughts that come into your
mind, but you can decide whether you will think on them. If there's
something on television that you don't want to watch, what do you

You can't always choose the thoughts that come into your mind, but you can decide whether you will think on them.

do? You either change the channel or turn off the TV. Do the same thing in your thought life. The moment a thought comes into your mind that is impure—maybe it's a past relationship or a man you find yourself admiring—banish it! Start thinking about something else. Philippians 4:8 says to think on things that are true, noble, right, pure, lovely, and admirable. If your thoughts don't fall into these categories, switch the channel.

A woman may find herself thinking about or admiring other men while her own husband goes weeks without a single word of admiration or encouragement from her. Find things in your husband that you appreciate and then verbally acknowledge them. You'll be surprised at what a difference it makes in both your lives.

Our Eyes

Choose wisely which TV shows and movies you watch. Many women admit to letting the lines blur in this regard. Watch how you speak and what you read. Many novels set up an unrealistic idea of what your life should be like. Many women's magazines do this as well.

Our Dress

Take care in how you dress. Seductive clothing is for your bedroom. Just as you want to protect your own thought life, you don't want to dress in a manner that will cause a man to struggle. A male friend at our church said recently, "I find it surprising how often I have to consciously choose to look away from how a woman is dressed, even at church. And I'm not just talking about how the teenage girls are dressing. I'm talking about women in their thirties, forties, and fifties."

Reverence

You are to feel for your husband all that reverence includes—to respect, defer to, revere him; (revere means) to honor, esteem, (appreciate, prize), and (in the human sense) adore him; (and adore means) to admire, praise, be devoted to, deeply love, and enjoy (your husband).[1]

Reverence is honor or respect, felt or shown. We will see that reverence has many aspects and we will address several of them here.

Reverence: To Respect

Respect: the special esteem or consideration in which one holds another person or thing.[2]

Survey after survey tells us that a woman's greatest desire in marriage is to feel loved by her husband, while a man's number one desire is to be respected by his wife. Respect must be one of the more difficult traits for wives to exhibit. Both Peter and Paul mention it: "And the wife must see to it that she respects her husband" (Ephesians 5:33, NASB).

A wife's respect is shown by highly regarding her husband. Often women withhold respect from their husbands, feeling that their husbands don't deserve it. "When he starts doing such and so," many women say, "then I'll give him my respect."

When a woman does this, what she is doing is *rewriting the Bible*. Notice that it doesn't say, "Wives, see to it that you respect your husbands *if they deserve it.*" It says, "Wives, see to it that you respect your husbands." It is a directive. Wives must choose whether they will respect their husbands. Do you respect your husband conditionally? Do you manipulate him to do certain things before you will give him your respect? Are you still waiting for him to change, thinking that then you will respect him? Remember, respect is not something your husband must earn from you. It is something you must give him because of the role God gave him.

There are small and large practical ways to demonstrate respect. One small courtesy is to give each other privacy in the bathroom at toilet time. Knock before entering, and ask your husband to do the same. Some women feel it's an indication of a good relationship when they and their husband can share the rest room when one of them is using the toilet. However, we believe this time should be kept personal and private since neither of you is at your best then.

More important, to show respect, give particular attention to your husband when he is talking. By doing this, you will be practicing something that is becoming rare in these fast-paced days: the art of listening.

A Lost Art

In our busy world, it seems that everyone is talking and no one is listening. But you can learn to develop your listening skills. Your objective is to draw the talker out, keeping attention away from yourself and on the other person.

"I had an interesting phone call today," says your husband.

Which response might draw him out?

1. "Tell me about it."
2. "So did I. My mother called and said…"

Here are seven tips to enhance your listening skills:

1. *Look at your husband when he speaks to you.* If your eyes are focused elsewhere, it will appear that your mind is as well. Stop whatever you're doing and look at your husband as he speaks.
2. *Lean forward as you listen.* Being on the "edge of your seat," with your body bent toward him as he speaks, shows him that you are very interested in what he is saying.
3. *Give feedback.* Respond to his words by nodding and smiling. Ask questions. This lets him know that you were listening closely to what he said.
4. *Don't interrupt or change the subject.* Wives are renowned for this! Let your husband finish his own sentences, and allow him to finish talking about the subject he's discussing, even if it's not your favorite. Don't yawn, look at your watch, or glance around the room.
5. *Repeat back to him some of the things he said.* This shows that you were listening and is validating and confirming.
6. *Acknowledge his insights and wisdom.* This will encourage him to continue sharing with you in the future.
7. *Show your appreciation.* Thank him for sharing his thoughts with you. Men are wired differently and often don't realize how much it means to a woman for her husband to talk to her.

Reverence: To Defer

Defer: allowing someone else's opinion and judgment to have more weight than one's own, willingly or politely.[3]

My (Nancy) sister Christine and I visit each other several times a year. It is delightful to spend time with her in Dallas. One of our favorite things to do is browse through the wonderful specialty stores near her home. On one such trip, Christine found a colorful rag rug for her kitchen. We both agreed it would fit perfectly and matched her kitchen.

We were right. It couldn't have looked more charming. We both loved the way it looked and couldn't wait to show it to Christine's husband.

When he came home that evening, he immediately told her that he couldn't stand the rug. He said it reminded him of his childhood poverty and the rugs his mother made from scraps because she could afford nothing better.

My sister gave me an unforgettable lesson in deference at this point. She simply said, "Well, darling, I'll take it back." Instead of a war of wills, instead of hurt feelings, Christine weighed the situation. She demonstrated that a rug is of little importance to her, whereas her relationship with her husband is vital.

Below are some other practical ways that a wife can defer to her husband:

1. Financial

One woman fought for years with her husband about how to invest their money. She liked the idea of insured deposits, while he liked the idea of the stock market. But after learning about deference in marriage, she chose to defer to her husband even though her mind remained unchanged regarding the investments. To her surprise, he frequently asked her opinion on things, eventually volunteering to keep as much in insured accounts as in the stock market!

This is not to say your finances will improve if you defer to your husband. If he's a poor money manager, you may lose money. Maybe living on your present income is a struggle and you feel that your husband is unwise in his spending. What do you do? You can appeal to him and give your input, but he alone is answerable to God for how he does things. Allow the final decision to be his, and leave the results to God.

2. Messy versus tidy

Many wives struggle with husbands who are messy, and they resent the dropped clothing, the dirty socks, the tools that are left lying hither and yon. One woman sought help from an older woman in the church.

"How much time would it take you if you picked up these things for your husband?" the older woman asked.

"Probably five or ten minutes a day."

"Wouldn't it be time well spent if you chose to serve your husband in this way instead of letting it eat away at you day after day?"

Some struggle with the opposite problem: husbands who are extremely tidy and fastidious. These women can choose to defer to their husbands by making a point of cheerfully keeping their things picked up and teaching their kids to do the same.

3. Personal preferences

Most men have opinions on things. Are we willing to respect these opinions when they are different from ours? This is a practical area where you can defer to your husband in a way that he will really appreciate.

Deferring to an Unwise Husband

Sometimes a wife is put in the position of having to defer to an unwise husband. How should she handle this? She can make suggestions that are well reasoned and openly discuss what she feels the ramifications might be. We share our opinions with our husbands, and through the years as we have grown in wisdom, our husbands have often asked for our opinions and followed our suggestions—but not always. We strive to accept their leadership.

If a husband's decision is immoral or goes against the teachings of God, a woman is not to defer to her husband. Her ultimate deference must be to Him. But if immorality or disobedience to God's law is not involved, then a woman should choose to defer to her husband. The bottom line is this: Your husband is responsible before God for his decisions—good or bad—and you have the protection of being in the will of God when you defer to him.

Reverence: To Revere

Revere: to regard with affectionate awe or veneration.[4]

Your husband is a man of great value to God. Jesus died for him and yearns to bring him into a right relationship with Himself. God has given him a special name: husband. Not to revere his God-given title is to damage your marriage. Marriage is God's idea, and He considers your relationship with your husband sacred and valuable.

How Long Has It Been?

How long has it been since you revered your husband? If you're like most women, the "dailyness" of life has a way of taking a toll, and it has probably been far too long. Too often we are left wondering why we ever held our husbands in awe in the first place.

Would you be willing to revere your husband once again? You may feel inadequately equipped to do so or that your husband is undeserving of your reverence. Don't worry! Be faithful in your attempt to introduce this concept into your marriage. God will bless your efforts as you begin afresh to revere your husband and the position of leadership in which he's been placed.

Regaining the Awe

You can begin to demonstrate to your husband that you revere him in many ways. If you're feeling stretched, that's good news! It shows that you're willing to change.

Do you feel like you need some help getting started? You might consider some of the following ideas:

- Regard him as worthy of great honor in the way you talk about him and to him. This is especially important before others: your children, your parents, friends, coworkers.
- Look at him with softness. My (Connie) husband has told me that he dislikes it when I look at him "that way" or give him "the look." A simple thing as how we look at our husbands conveys volumes concerning our thoughts about them.
- Try making phone calls when he isn't home, and take only emergency calls when he is home. I (Nancy) make a point of doing this, and my husband appreciates it immensely. Friends thought this quite strange in the beginning, but many now do the same thing.
- Consistently prepare something he likes for dinner and serve him the choicest portion. When we began doing this, our children loved it. They greatly enjoyed seeing us treat their fathers in this way.

Reverence: To Honor

Honor: to treat with respect, honor, regard; one whose worth brings respect.[5]

Over forty years ago, at Fuchu Air Force Base in Tokyo, Japan, I (Nancy) was the secretary who recorded the testimony at the court-martial of a sergeant. The charge against him was that he didn't maintain order in his home. In reality, it was his wife who did not tend her home and children when her husband was at work. By all accounts, when the sergeant was home things ran smoothly. Tragically, he was reduced in rank and had to leave the Air Force because his lowered salary could not support his family.

A wife must maintain her husband's good name, public esteem, and reputation. Not to do so reflects poorly on her husband and in some cases can affect his employment.

Ways to Honor Your Husband

A wife can honor her husband by:

- Making sure her own behavior is beyond reproach. A woman's behavior affects how others see her husband.
- Not dishonoring his name in any way. "Husband bashing" has become far too common when women get together. It's one thing to bring your personal problems before a trusted Christian counselor, pastor, or friend; it's quite another to share your husband's faults with casual or even close friends. Also, be cautious with prayer requests. Not every Christian keeps a confidence.
- Remembering that if you are married to a Christian man, you are married to someone of highest worth to Christ. If Christ regards your husband as precious and worthy, how can you possibly not? A woman who is married to a non-Christian should treat her husband in the same way. Christ died for his sins as well and desires a relationship with him. First Peter

3:1–2 says that a wife's behavior could be the vessel used to win a non-Christian husband to Christ.

- Asking yourself whether your children see you honoring their father. You greatly influence how they view their father by how you honor him.
- Remembering that honor involves all you do with your life— the way you talk and work, the values you hold, your morals. Everything you do, say, watch, or read involves honor.

Are you bringing honor to God in the way you treat your husband? We are to "love each other with brotherly affection and *take delight* in honoring each other" (Romans 12:10, TLB). Are you taking delight in honoring your husband?

Reverence: To Adore

Adore (in the human sense): to regard with loving devotion by giving time, effort, and care.[6]

In the last six years of her life, my (Nancy) mother was almost totally restricted to her bedroom because of emphysema. My dad began to sleep on a couch in her room to be near her and tend to her needs. After four years of caregiving, Dad, in his late seventies, needed some help. So he and Mom left their home in Texas and moved to ours in North Carolina. I watched his continual devotion to his beloved Teresa. I could help during the day, but at night he took over all her needs, sleeping on a daybed in her room.

Toward the end, as Mom grew weaker, she couldn't leave her bed. Dad remained her constant companion, prioritizing her over all else. He oversaw the distribution of her medication and attended to her oxygen machine. He was in his early eighties, and all of this took a toll on him.

The night Mom died, I remember coming downstairs around midnight and hearing sounds of troubled breathing. I tiptoed into their room, and there, resting at the foot of her bed, was my faithful father.

This time, as we struggled to help her, we knew the time had come for her to leave behind the trials of this world. As my father sat with his arms around her, she slipped into the presence of Jesus.

This is devotion. This is adoration in the human sense. Did Mom appreciate this? She once confided to me that her last years were the happiest of her life! How she loved Dad!

God did the dearest thing for my father. Dad bought the home in which he was born ninety years ago in Virginia. He lived there alone for eleven years, surrounded by pictures of Mom. He played tennis three times a week and walked several miles a day. He looked years younger than his age, until the day he died. I think it was God saying, "Well done, good and faithful servant."

How devoted are you to your husband?

Not Too Late to Begin

After twenty-five years of marriage, one woman we know decided this sounded like a challenge worth trying. She began noticing what her husband liked, what he needed, and what pleased him. He blossomed with all this new attention, and she began loving him in a brand-new way.

Not too long ago, he exuberantly declared, "Coming home to you is like going to a five-star resort. Whenever I sit in my chair at night, I feel like I'm sitting in first class."

Try adoring your husband and see what happens!

Are we getting carried away? Most women find it easy to adore special people and various things. One woman we know said she adored her kids, fun friends, fabulous restaurants, and clothes that made her look like she had a waistline. When asked if she adored her husband, she was shocked!

"Surely you're joking," she said incredulously. "Grown women don't adore their husbands."

"Why not?" we asked.

"I don't know," she said, a bit perplexed. "We just don't. We respect them and love them, but adore them? Plus I'm not sure mine would want to be adored. He'd say that was a feminine thing."

We challenged this woman to go home and ask her husband how he would feel about her adoring him. So she did. Without any explanation, she asked simply, "Do you think you'd like it if I adored you?"

"Absolutely."

"Are you kidding?" she responded, giving him a chance to rethink his quick answer.

"No, I'm not kidding," he assured her. "There's not a man I can think of who wouldn't love being adored by his wife."

Reverence: To Admire

Admire: to marvel; to wonder; to astonish; to be delighted by.[7]

To admire your husband is one of the most powerful things you can do for him. It is so potent that you must do it wisely and without manipulation. Most men prefer being admired to being loved. If you doubt

Most men prefer being admired to being loved.

this, tell your husband that you love him and study his reaction. Then, after prayerful consideration, think of something you admire about him. Say to him, "There is something about you that I truly admire." Watch his attentiveness. You will be amazed at how powerful words of admiration are to your husband.

Would you consider saying to your husband tonight, "There is something about you I truly admire"? Then share it with him. Lay your discomfort aside. Swallow your pride if you need to. Ask God for a spirit of humility and sincerity. Then step out in faith and tell your husband you admire him. You can do it! And God will bless you in your efforts.

Focus on His Strengths

Most men appreciate being admired physically. What do you admire about his body? Maybe his brute strength? Maybe his long legs or strong arms? One man we know wears his hair a certain way because his wife has told him how much she likes it. You could admire your husband's lovemaking skills—his gentleness or sensitivity.

Sometimes a woman will consider traits she had once admired in her husband as faults or flaws. My (Nancy) husband, Ray, is direct, blunt, and to the point. He is honorable and honest. He says what he thinks and means what he says. He doesn't sugarcoat his conversations. It was one of the things about him that attracted me to him. As time passed, however, I began to view his manner of speech as rather rude and unfriendly. Without conscious thought, or his asking or desiring my assistance, I decided to help him overcome this. The stress this created in me lasted for years until I realized what I was doing. I began to notice the wise counsel he gave to our children. They might not always appreciate the way he makes his point, but they deeply appreciate his insight, and so do I.

Now I seldom offer advice on how he expresses himself—he doesn't need it. Far too few people say what they think. I once again see this as a strength and admire it in my husband.

Advice Worth Remembering

A friend who is a counselor once said, "Most frequently it is not a younger woman, or a more beautiful woman, or a thinner woman that captures a married man's attention, but it is an admiring woman. Few women realize just how powerful words of admiration are to a man. Wives would be wise to remember that this is an area in which they can tremendously impact their husbands. If he is admired in his own home, he is much less likely to go looking for it someplace else."

Reverence: To Praise

Praise: to express approval; to commend.[8]

How good it feels to be praised! We praise our children for learning new skills or bringing home an A paper from school. We praise our friends for losing weight, for hosting a successful luncheon, or for making a difficult decision. We praise our pets for their loyalty and eagerness to please us. We even praise total strangers whom we will most likely never see again. But rare is the woman who praises her husband.

Praise, like admiration, is a powerful thing to a man. Regardless of their temperament, education, income, or anything else, men desire to hear words of praise from their wives. Too often the words of praise that overflow in relationships in early years turn into words of criticism and harshness.

But the good news is that praise can be reintroduced into a marriage at any time! It is one of the simplest things to do. Here are some tips to get you started:

1. Try noticing the things he does and let him know that you notice.
2. If he does something for you, don't criticize the way he does it.
3. If he buys you an orange robe for Christmas, resist the urge to immediately ask whether or not he kept the sales receipt.
4. Comment on the yard when he mows it. If he doesn't mow it, don't mention repeatedly that you greatly admire your neighbor for mowing his so faithfully.
5. Thank him for filling your car with gasoline, having the oil changed, checking the tires, or anything else he does for you in this regard.

Everyone is different! A dear older friend once said that she was horrified when she called her married daughter and asked what she was doing. "I'm mowing the lawn," the daughter said.

"Why are you mowing the lawn? Shouldn't Bob be doing that?"

"No." The daughter laughed. "I'm mowing the lawn, and he's cooking a fabulous dinner."

Be creative and thoughtful about how you can sincerely praise your husband. Don't make any announcements or create such an issue of it that the attention actually falls on you.

Also, don't use guilt, manipulation, or nagging to get your husband to do something so you can praise him. Maybe your husband does very little for you. Frequently men say they don't do things because their wives will criticize the way they did them. Are you guilty of this? The husband in one couple we know arranged a getaway weekend as a surprise for his wife. The wife was upset when she discovered that they weren't staying at a certain hotel, and she told him repeatedly of her disappointment. The weekend was ruined for both of them, and her husband stopped thinking of ways to surprise her.

It is generally believed that for every negative statement someone makes, anywhere from seven to ten positive statements are needed to counteract the negative words. Every time you tell your husband he did something wrong, you need seven to ten opportunities to tell him he did something right to offset the negative comments.

Reverence: To Love Deeply

Love deeply: a profound, powerful emotion felt for another person.[9]

There is a program on television that chronicles the courtship and marriage of couples. Since marriage is a subject I (Nancy) care deeply about, I have watched it occasionally with much interest and intrigue. I find it fascinating to see why couples choose to marry each other. Without exception, the couples express deep love for each other and freely convey their reasons for marrying. I know from statistics that half of these couples will divorce, one can spot the red flag statements that could spell trouble as time goes by. One starry-eyed new husband said that he loved his wife because she had never let him down. She replied that she loved him because he loved *her* so much, and she didn't think anyone else in the world would ever love her like that.

What will happen when she lets him down, as she will surely do at some point? Will he love her less and thus negate the very reason she chose him?

176   The Politically Incorrect Wife

"I love him because he is so handsome, tender, spontaneous, helpful, interesting…."

You can probably recall your own reasons for marriage. The ones we've listed, however, do not define the highest love one person can have for another. That love is holier and stronger. The love you are to have for your husband is the kind that doesn't run out. You don't fall out of true love because you don't fall into true love— *you choose to love.*

Love is a choice you make to be primarily concerned with the well-being of another, regardless of his reaction or condition. This is agape love—the love Jesus has for you. Jesus said, "Love one another, even as I have loved you…. By this all men will know that you are My disciples" (John 13:34–35, NASB).

You show this kind of love to your husband by being unselfishly loyal to him. Hold him dear. Respond to his lovemaking. Show him how much he means to you with both words and actions. Tell him you love him and demonstrate it at every opportunity.

Suppose you don't feel in love with your husband? As we discussed earlier, act the way you want to feel. Your feelings will catch up with your actions.

Cold, Indifferent Husbands

Some men have grown cold toward their wives and may shun them no matter what they say or do. How can a woman show love to her husband in that case? By her behavior, empowered by the Holy Spirit. By patiently, steadfastly demonstrating her love in every way. Jesus loved those who were cool to Him, even those who hated Him. He loves you and me, and we are not always lovable. We grow cool to Him at times, yet He continues to love us. Ask Him to work through you, to enable you to show love to a husband that has grown cold. Ask Him to love your husband through you.

Reverence: To Enjoy

Enjoy: to rejoice over; to have a good time with; to take pleasure or satisfaction in.[10]

If you were asked to list several things in life that you enjoy, what would you place on that list? An unexpected note from a friend? A warm spring day? A relaxing evening spent with those closest to you?

Would your husband's name appear on the list?

A simple way to enjoy your husband is to do special things for him. Ray treasures the simple things in life and appreciates every effort I (Nancy) make to please him, even if he doesn't always say so. For him, special things might include:

- Coffee in bed
- Setting aside time to trim his hair (I learned to do this practicing on our sons when they didn't know how hair was supposed to look!)
- A seafood dinner, preferably fried, or banana pudding like his mom used to make
- Watching the Nebraska Cornhuskers play football (especially if they're winning)
- A surprise gift from his favorite store
- Exclaiming over his freshly mowed lawn as I bring him ice water and a cool, wet towel
- Planning a trip to see our children
- Catching a matinee at the movies

Consider giving your husband small presents or surprises. We know of one husband who suddenly discovered hair growing on his ears, as is the tendency as men age. His wife found a personal grooming kit at a local department store. It was small and inexpensive and had special scissors that were made for clipping those wandering hairs. She purchased the kit and put it in her husband's drawer. No words were ever spoken, but she could sense his appreciation and love when he discovered it.

It doesn't take a lot of time, effort, or money to let your husband know that you enjoy him and want to do things for him. If your husband likes a certain kind of cookie, slip a bag of them into his suitcase on his next trip. Discover what his interests are and become involved.

If there's something he *dislikes,* don't insist that he do it. I (Connie) love to go for drives. My family did this when I was growing up, and it was a special time for all of us. However, my husband considers them a waste of time. Early in our marriage, I was determined that he would enjoy these drives as much as I did. "Just give them a chance," I would say in exasperation.

"Drives are not relaxing to me," he'd reply. "Drop me off at home first, and then go on your drive."

Where's his sense of fun? I'd think. Finally it dawned on me that it was okay if he didn't want to go. What if he insisted I do something I disliked? I wouldn't appreciate it, yet that's exactly what I was doing to him. I quit lecturing and cajoling and started taking drives when he was working or tied up with something else.

The Time Is Now!

Do you find that you just don't have time to enjoy your husband? Try to figure out a way to build this into your schedule. Life is too short to wait. Take a lesson from a good friend of ours whose husband died while still in his forties. Although they had twenty wonderful years together, she says, "I wish I had enjoyed him more when he was living. Life was usually so busy and frantic that we didn't take time for each other, especially after the kids came. We put our relationship on hold, thinking that one day the kids would be gone and then there would be time for us again. We were wrong. He was gone before the kids were."

Think of a way to let your husband know that you enjoy him, and then do it. We believe it is something you will never regret.

POSTSCRIPT

This chapter has been chock-full of information, instruction, and ideas. Perhaps you are mulling over some of what you've learned, or maybe you've already begun to introduce some of these principles into your marriage.

In talking with dozens of women who are attempting to do what you have just read about, a question comes up over and over: When will my husband start doing his part?

Most women are willing to put these principles to work in their marriages—up to a point. They begin and the first few days fly by quickly. Because the wives are still excited and motivated, the next few weeks speed by as well. Before long, though, fatigue begins to set in. They expect or hope that their husbands will notice their efforts, which might not happen. Their resolve weakens, yet they continue on, albeit at a slower pace. Before long their energies fail. The excitement ebbs. They begin to ask themselves, *Wouldn't it be a good idea if someone taught my husband what his responsibilities are?*

They are tired of doing all the work. They become worn out and discouraged.

"If only my husband would do just a portion of what I'm doing, I could keep going," said one woman. "But he's not doing a thing. And he's not even noticing my efforts. If he's not going to notice, I'm going to save myself the trouble. I am no longer going to do this." And so she stopped.

Don't let her story be yours as well. Don't stop! Don't "save yourself the trouble." What you are doing isn't trouble. What you are doing is God's will!

One young woman we know began incorporating many of these things into her marriage. It was exciting for the first three weeks, but then she began to have second thoughts. Her old way of life felt more comfortable and, as she told us, "I thought to myself, *Why should I do all these things for him?*"

Just then her three-year-old daughter came into the room. She told her child, "It's time to brush your teeth."

To which her daughter replied, "Why should I?"

Why should I?

Mothers, could it be that one reason your children are not obeying you is that you are not obeying what your heavenly Father tells you to do? Are you reaping what you sow?

Don't let your motive for doing this be *only* because you want your husband to notice, or your marriage to change, or your life to get better. Do this because it brings honor and glory to Jesus Christ. If your husband notices, great! If he doesn't, that's fine too. You are not doing it because of him. You're doing it because of *Him*. The key is to stop focusing on yourself and start focusing on Jesus Christ and your role.

Honestly ask yourself whether you are doing this...

For yourself?

For your husband?

For your kids?

Or for the Lord?

HOW ABOUT YOU?

Are you willing to apply these principles—but only up to a point? At what point will you decide to go back to your old ways of disobeying the Lord?

Don't be an "up to a point" kind of woman. Don't be just a starter—be a finisher! Don't quit the work God has called you to do.

The Bible tells us that after Peter denied Jesus for the third time, Jesus turned and looked into his eyes, and Peter went outside and wept bitterly. One day Jesus will look into your eyes. You will give an account to Him of how you have lived your life. What will you say in the area of being a godly wife? Will it be a joyful recollection, or will it be filled with sorrow and regret? Will it be joy? Or will it be shame? The choice is yours, and you can bring glory to God by the choice you make.

Chapter Seven: Who Says Beauty Is Only Skin Deep?

The world today puts tremendous emphasis on external appearances. People flock to gyms in droves, searching for better bodies. Imaginary stairs are climbed and bicycles going nowhere are pedaled madly. Women sweat to the oldies and the not-so-oldies. *Surely if we work a little harder,* we think, *we can be ten pounds thinner by summer.* Cosmetic sales are soaring, and age-defying products are flying off of the shelves as never before. We have become a nation bent on maintaining youth and beauty at all costs. This is especially true for women.

An overabundance of material tells us that if we are outwardly attractive we are more valuable, more desirable, and more respectable. A recent ad in a women's magazine touted makeup as a woman's most important accessory.

We agree completely. A woman's make-up is the most important thing about her, period. Her *inner make-up,* that is. We call this "holy beauty." It is not based on the world's standard of beauty; it is based on the Lord's standard. It is a beauty that God calls unfading, and we are told in His Word how we can have it. It doesn't have to be wiped on, rubbed in, ripped off, or reapplied in the morning. It is a twenty-four-hour-a-day beauty package, and it can be yours if you're willing to obey God's Word.

Holy beauty…God's idea of beautiful!

Who Says Beauty Is Only Skin Deep?

She is forever beautiful, the one who resembles Christ.

*S*he was barely five feet tall and had to stretch to see above the steering wheel when she drove. Her hair was a beautiful silver-gray, her face caressed with wrinkles. Joy danced in her eyes, and she spoke with a lilt in her voice. She was so magnetic, yet her life seemed so ordinary. What made her the way she was? I (Connie) couldn't quite figure it out. I was a young girl, and she was my great-aunt.

When I was nine, she gave me a Bible with my name inscribed on the front in gold lettering. Up to this time, I had shared a Bible with my sisters. Now I had my very own. I was so proud! She told me it was the greatest book I would ever own. Just the way she held it in her hands told me she dearly loved it.

Like my family, she lived on a farm, which was only a few miles from us. She had made the country house charming. The single bathroom, with a clawfoot tub, was accessible only by first walking through two bedrooms. The kitchen was small, but oh, the generosity and love that could be felt when a special treat or meal was shared with a guest. Every time we visited, announced or unannounced, we received a grand welcome. "You've just made my day," she'd say cheerfully. "How kind of you to visit. Come in!"

My great-aunt knew hard times and heartache, but she bore no ill will or bitterness. These were foreign words to her. She loved to attend church, but her husband was not a churchgoing man. Never do I recall her complaining or wishing aloud to my mother (when we girls were listening from an adjoining room) that he would go with her. "He's in God's hands," she'd say. She loved him with a loyalty and fervor that was rare even then. She treated him as a prized jewel, although he wasn't one to display such emotion in return. She didn't gossip or judge, and she had a way about her that made you want to behave in the same manner.

I observed all of this for some time and even as a young girl knew she was special. Although she lived an everyday kind of life—her world humble, her days predictable—she radiated something that made me want what she had.

It would be years before I realized what it was that made her so special. She had committed her life to Jesus and lived it trying to be like Him. Because of that, she had been transformed from the inside out. *She was holy beautiful.* What I had observed for years was a reflection of what He had done in her life. Her beauty came straight from the Maker Himself. No wonder I was so attracted to her.

Holy beauty, unlike external beauty, never fades, and is, in fact, enhanced with each passing year. It's the ultimate beauty product and is produced in us by God Himself. That's what we'll be discussing in this chapter, but first we'll look briefly at external beauty.

EXTERNAL BEAUTY

Say what you will, a woman's external appearance is important to her husband. A friend of ours says, "If you ask one hundred men if their wife's appearance matters to them, ninety-five of them will say yes, and the other five won't have understood the question!"

When I (Nancy) was a little girl, my mother would actually change her clothes and mine before Dad came home. Somehow that heightened the anticipation of his arrival. She wanted us to look nice when he came home from his workday, and he always seemed to appreciate that she did this.

In many households today, both the husband and wife work outside the home. We believe that all women are working women—whether in the home, out of the home, or both. Every woman's role is vital and touches dozens of lives around her. How much time you have to freshen up at the end of the day depends on your personal circumstances. Some women have ample opportunity to do this, while some don't. Regardless, it is a fortunate man who has a wife who makes an effort to look nice for him.

A Man's Perspective

It's a well-known fact that men are more visual than women. It is one of the ways we're different. If you show a man a picture of an attractive woman, frequently his eyes will linger. If you show a woman a picture of a nice-looking man, often his appearance won't even register in her mind.

I (Connie) remember visiting a newlywed couple many years ago. We decided to drive to the ice cream shop for dessert. The wife ordered two scoops of vanilla. Her husband suggested she get just one. She assured him she wanted two. He assured her he thought one was more than enough. After energetically discussing the issue for a few moments, she left the store without buying anything.

We saw these friends recently and laughed at the memory. Our friend readily admitted that he was attempting to make certain that his wife's physical appearance stayed the same following the wedding. "I hope I no longer try to control her like that," he said, "but I can't say enough about how much I appreciate her staying in shape after all these years. I think if any man were honest, he'd say that his wife's physical appearance matters greatly to him."

Most men wish they were able to see beyond the external to the internal, but few are able to do so.

It's frustrating to many women that men place such a high value on external appearances. To a woman, this seems superficial and relatively unimportant. It's difficult for her to understand why this often seems to carry as much or more weight with her husband than her inner beauty.

We talked to several men to glean insight into this matter. Their opinions, though varied, all came down to the same basic conclusion: Most men wish they *were* able to see beyond the external to the internal, but few are able to do so. As one man said, "I don't know why men are so visually stimulated. I'd like to say I'm not, but I am! I know this sounds awfully shallow, but that's the way it is. I'm in a large Bible study, and it's an issue for every man in the group. We've talked about it many times. It is an ongoing struggle, and temptation is never far away, even for godly men. Not the temptation to fall into adultery, perhaps, but certainly the temptation to look too long or imagine too much. You can hardly go to your mailbox anymore without this issue hitting you in the face.

"It makes a world of difference to a man when his wife *makes an effort* to look nice for him. To a man, this shows love, care, and respect for him. Men see their wives as a reflection of themselves. We're around well-dressed women all day in the workplace. To come home to a woman who is disheveled and unkempt is not something any man I know looks forward to. I think if wives realized how important this is to their husbands, they might consider changing."

This can be a difficult issue for a man to broach with his wife. One man said, "I don't mention this issue anymore because my wife becomes extremely defensive and argumentative. She accuses me of not loving the 'real' her. In an effort to keep the peace, I no longer bring it up. However, my desire for her to look nice hasn't changed. The only thing that has changed is that it's no longer verbalized. It's still an issue to me, just an unspoken one."

Most men care how their wives look, whether they say it or not. A wise woman would consider giving some thought to this and asking God if she needs to work on this. Without making any announcements, you might begin to make improvements. Do it with a joyful, glad heart, and don't get discouraged if he doesn't say anything. Many times it is awkward for a husband to say much, especially if there's been conflict in the past. Not only will you enjoy doing this for your husband, but many women find this makes them feel better about themselves as well.

Exercise

Is exercise part of your schedule? Women are busier than ever before and think they don't have time for exercise, yet often exercise actually gives them a renewed sense of energy. Most experts recommend exercising for twenty to thirty minutes at least three times a week. Exercise is both physically and emotionally good for you.

Some women get up early to fit exercise into their schedules. Many have found that it helps to exercise with a partner or in a group. This provides companionship as well as accountability. One woman we know walks every morning and uses this time to pray and reflect on the Lord. Is exercising a must for the godly woman? No! Some women are physically unable to exercise. But for those of you who are able, you might find it beneficial.

Other Ideas

The ways for a woman to care for her external appearance are innumerable. Magazines are replete with simple tips. Fix your hair in a flattering way. If you don't have much time, find a low maintenance cut that works well for you. You can wear inexpensive jewelry to offset your clothes, or you might find a scarf that makes an outfit really shine. There is a huge assortment of women's clothes to choose from these days, clothes that fit all sizes and budgets. Both of us frequent consignment shops and find things that work for us at a fraction of their retail prices. A minimal amount of makeup can go a long way in making you look your best and takes just moments to apply.

Have you noticed that when you wear an old shirt with paint stains and your husband's oversize sweatpants, you actually *feel* tired? Try taking the time to dress for your day, and don't sacrifice looking nice for comfort. It's easy to have both. Most women wear 20 percent of their clothing 80 percent of the time. Find clothes that work for you and that you can see yourself wearing immediately. If you catch yourself thinking *I'll probably wear this sometime* when you're considering purchasing an item, chances are you won't! Put it back on the rack and find something that you'll wear often. It doesn't take long to distinguish between what you'll wear often and what you'll hardly wear.

A Surprise Party

I'll (Nancy) never forget attending a "come as you are" birthday party. The women who planned the event had selected several drivers to pick up the invited women around 9:30 P.M.

I was quite surprised when our doorbell rang. We had just put our four young children to bed. When I answered the door, I had only enough time to grab my purse before being whisked away to the hostess's home.

About twenty women had been invited, and we knew one another well. What fun it was for us to suddenly find ourselves out for an impromptu evening. As we talked about our rapid getaways, we began to look at each other. Normally at such a gathering, we all looked our best. But not that night! Most of us were embarrassed. Traces of lipstick gave evidence of faces that had been fussed over much earlier. Almost everyone's hair had not seen a brush in hours. And where in the world did we get those old sweatpants, unmatched tops, and ragged bathrobes? After perusing one another's outfits, our eyes rested on one friend in particular, and the questions began:

"You knew about this, didn't you?" we said in chorus.

"No!" she exclaimed. "Why would you think that?"

"Because you look so nice. Your hair is in place, you're wearing a matching outfit, and you have on fresh lipstick. You look better than we do when we're getting ready to leave the house!"

"Really, I didn't know!" We weren't convinced. Obviously, she took far more care with her dress at home than the rest of us did.

Blessed is the husband whose wife pays attention to the way she looks for his sake, as well as her own.

The woman commended in Proverbs 31 wore good clothes—fine linen and purple (v. 22, NASB). However, this is not to be the focal point of who you are. More important than this by far is the hidden person of your heart.

INNER BEAUTY

> Let it be the inward adorning and beauty of the hidden person of the heart, with the incorruptible and unfading charm of a gentle and peaceful spirit, which (is not anxious or wrought up, but) is very precious in the sight of God. (1 Peter 3:4, AMP)

What makes a woman beautiful? It is the imperishable quality of a gentle and quiet spirit. A time will come when your physical beauty will fade. A time will also come when your sexuality is not as enticing to your husband as it is now. What are you doing now to prepare for these future changes? Are you allowing God to develop your *inner beauty*?

How can you develop the qualities of a gentle and quiet spirit? By *cultivating* them.

A Gentle Spirit

What does it mean to be gentle? One of the definitions may surprise you: to belong to a family of high station, of noble birth.[1]

It is incredible to realize that a Christian is of noble birth, born into the family of God.

To be gentle is to be free of harshness, sternness, and violence. Do you scream at your children or husband? Do you have a quick temper? Try softening your voice—it's surprising to see a child respond to the whispers of his mother and a husband blossom because of a soft-spoken wife.

Choose to be a gentlewoman! Here's our definition of such a person: one who is born again and is submissive to and surrendered to the lordship of Christ.

Jesus was gentle and humble in heart (Matthew 11:29, NASB). Don't you want to become like Him? The more you learn about Jesus and surrender to Him, the more this will happen.

A Quiet Spirit

Peacefulness is becoming a valuable commodity in our culture. Have you noticed that it is for sale these days? Aromatherapy, candles, soaps, creams, and elixirs all claim to be the antidote for stress. Small, soft, lavender-scented pillows or bedside machines that mimic the sounds of waves, rain, birds, and wind are helping the sleeping habits of the restless.

But what can compare to a *spirit that is peaceful,* not anxious or overwrought? No price tag can be put on a soul that is tranquil, calm, and still—free from noise or uproar. That comes from having a right relationship with God, which is freely offered by Him.

> Peace I leave with you. My peace I give to you; not as the world gives do I give to you. Do not let your heart be troubled, nor let it be fearful. (John 14:27, NASB)

Here are some simple, practical things a woman can do to maintain a quiet spirit:

- Start the day with prayer.
- Spend time with and abide in Christ.
- Ask for God's help in developing a quiet spirit.
- Grocery shop for a week with a complete list.
- Don't go to bed, if possible, with the kitchen and living areas unsightly. (This causes you to begin the next day behind schedule.)
- Watch your caffeine and sugar intake.
- Don't overcommit yourself.
- Don't sign your children up for too many after-school activities.
- Plan for a day at home—we call them "home days"—and put it on the calendar.
- Don't overspend.
- Try to fold the laundry as it comes out of the dryer. This can be a real time-saver.
- Take a bubble bath. You can purchase a small tub pillow to lean against; read an uplifting book as you soak.
- Put the children to bed earlier.
- Play praise music.
- Ask your husband to massage your shoulders and neck; offer to do this for him if he enjoys it.
- Forgive quickly; don't bear grudges.

A Hopeful Spirit

For in this way in former times the holy women also, who
hoped in God, used to adorn themselves, being submissive
to their own husbands. (1 Peter 3:5, NASB)

Your hope in God is a necessary part of developing inner
beauty. To be holy beautiful, you must believe in God and also hope

in Him. Hope is to "cherish a desire with anticipation and to expect with confidence and trust that God is working on your behalf."[2]

Sarah placed her hope in God. How wise she was, and what a leap of faith her life demonstrates to us. For ninety years she was childless, and she had come to deeply regret her own plan that Abraham have a child with her maid, Hagar (Genesis 16:1–16). Then one day the Lord appeared to Abraham and told him that the next year Sarah would have a son. Sarah laughed when she heard this, saying, "After I have become old, shall I have pleasure, my lord being old also?" After the Lord Himself confronted her, revealing to her that He knew her thoughts, Sarah's faith was born (Genesis 18:1–15, NASB). She placed her hope and faith in God and considered Him faithful to do what He had promised. And what God had promised came to be, just as He said it would: Sarah gave birth to Isaac.

Sarah is an example of a woman who obeyed her husband and responded to him as the leader of her household. And God considered this so noteworthy that He put her in His "Hall of Fame" as one who triumphed in her faith (Hebrews 11).

Where do you place your hope? Sarah placed hers in God, expectantly and with confidence. She knew God would do as He said even though she had not conceived a child as a young woman. It would seem she anticipated that God would work on her behalf even in the most difficult circumstances.

The Key

Peter, who gives us Sarah as an example, tells us:

> You are now her true daughters if you do right and let nothing terrify you—not giving way to hysterical fears or letting anxieties unnerve you. (1 Peter 3:6, AMP)

Fearlessness seems to be intertwined with a woman's choice to acknowledge her husband's leadership. If you are a fearful person, ask yourself, "Have I taken the leadership of the home away from my husband and neglected verbal and heartfelt acknowledgment that my husband is responsible *before God* to be the leader?"

To take over the leadership in the home, it seems to us, results in emotional unrest and fearfulness in the heart of a wife.

Are You a Controlling Woman?

In a recent discussion, a woman confessed to being a "control freak." As she described herself and her controlling ways, she acknowledged that she had indeed become a very anxious woman. Examine yourself if you are fearful. Could it be that you need to give back the leadership role in your family to your husband?

This involves a conscious decision on your part. Once you do this, don't use "constructive" criticism or second-guess your husband. If you've led the family for any length of time, give him a while to hit his stride. Encourage him! Both of you will be blessed by God as you fulfill your roles. Remember, your hope is in God, not in your husband and his abilities.

A Considerate Spirit

In the same way you married men should live considerately with [your wives], with an intelligent recognition [of the marriage relation] honoring the woman as [physically] the weaker, but [realizing that you] are joint heirs of the grace (God's unmerited favor) of life, in order that your prayers may not be hindered and cut off. —Otherwise you cannot pray effectively. (1 Peter 3:7, AMP)

It seems to us that a woman can help her husband in this regard. How can she do this?

She can choose behavior that her husband will respect. She can be cooperative and pleasant. A friend recently said to us, "I don't know if my wife knows how much I love her, but I know for certain how much she loves me because of the way she treats me." This same man, at a Valentine's Day banquet, was asked to list ten things he valued in his wife. His number one reason: "I love the way she loves me." What a fortunate man! And what a godly woman! Surely that's the way God intended it to be. Even if a wife fails to do this, it is still the husband's responsibility to love his wife. There will come a day when he will answer to God regarding this issue.

Can you imagine what your home life would become if both of you respected, loved, and supported each other—even if one of you were having a bad day?

THE ROAD THAT MATTERS

Regardless of where your marriage is at this point, you are in the place of blessing when you choose to do what is right. One aspect of doing so is striving to have a harmonious home. Peter sums up what he has been saying:

> Finally, all of you, live in harmony with one another; be sympathetic, love as brothers, be compassionate and humble. (1 Peter 3:8)

These virtues are Jesus' own character. He lives in you and can exhibit these traits through you.

Loving the Unlovable

It is easy to live in harmony when your husband is treating you well. But what if he's not? How do you treat your husband when he is unloving and moody? Listen to what Jesus says regarding difficult relationships:

> "Love your enemies. Let them bring out the best in you, not the worst. When someone gives you a hard time, respond with the energies of prayers for that person…. If someone takes unfair advantage of you, use the occasion to practice the servant life. No more tit-for-tat stuff. Live generously.
>
> "Here is a simple rule of thumb for your behavior: Ask yourself what you want people to do for you; then grab the initiative and do it for *them!* If you only love the lovable, do you expect a pat on the back?… I tell you, love your enemies. Help and give without expecting a return. You'll never—I promise—regret it. Live out this God-created identity the way our Father lives toward us, generously and graciously, even when we're at our worst. Our Father is kind; you be kind.
>
> "Don't pick on people, jump on their failures, criticize their faults—unless, of course, you want the same treatment. Don't condemn those who are down; that hardness can boomerang. Be easy on people; you'll find life a lot easier. Give away your life; you'll find life given back, but not merely given back—given back with bonus and blessing. Giving, not getting, is the way. Generosity begets generosity."
> (Luke 6:27–38, *The Message*)

One way you can tell that you are walking in the Spirit in your marriage is to ask: Is my husband's response my goal, or am I doing this to please the Lord?

God will enable you to be compassionate to someone who doesn't deserve it, just as He was and is to you.

Ask yourself, "Why is my husband moody and sharp with me?" Often the answer is that you are simply catching the overflow of what happened to him at work, with his parents, or with some other problem. *Is this fair?* No, but life isn't always fair. Consider other possibilities as well: Is he stressed about something in particular? Is he fatigued due to extra hours he's putting in at work? Is he going through a difficult time with someone? Ask God to give you understanding and patience during these times and continue to treat your husband lovingly, regardless of how he may be treating you.

Don't be so sensitive that you let your feelings and emotions be set by another's treatment of you. Jesus didn't do that. He continued to live His life with honor, dignity, love, and mercy through the most difficult times. Don't be judgmental or unfriendly. Don't allow yourself to be too easily wounded, crushed, or hurt. Guard against bitterness by being quick to forgive. Ask Jesus to help develop these attitudes in you when you face challenging times.

Be a Blessing

Your job is to bless (1 Peter 3:9, *The Message*). Put another way, it reads like this:

> Never return evil for evil or insult for insult—scolding, tongue-lashing, berating; but on the contrary blessing—

praying for their welfare, happiness, and protection, and
truly pitying and loving them. For *know that* to this you
have been called, that you may yourselves inherit a blessing [from God]— obtain a blessing as heirs, bringing welfare and happiness and protection. (1 Peter 3:9, AMP)

Holy, beautiful women never return harsh words, but instead
give a blessing back! One way to do this is through prayer. Do you
see that the blessed outcome of our unselfish prayer for our husbands' welfare, happiness, and protection is that we inherit these
things as well?

Have you and your husband ever been in the following cycle? He
raises his voice; you raise yours. He becomes louder; you retaliate.

This is an endless cycle, but the dynamics of it can be broken
quickly if you no longer react. You can choose to act instead in a

You can choose to
no longer react, but
to act instead in a
manner the Bible
says is right.

manner the Bible says is right. Your consis-
tent, sweet, silent response to poor behavior
may be the very thing God uses to change
your husband. Don't give in to the urge to let
your silence be cold and stony.

When Jesus was oppressed and afflicted,
He did not open His mouth (Isaiah 53:7;
Matthew 26:63; 27:12–14, NASB). Mark says
that Pilate was amazed at how Jesus stayed
silent in the midst of the accusations that were swirling around
Him. Only when He was placed under oath and asked whether He
was the King of the Jews did He humbly reply, "Yes, it is as you say"
(Mark 15:2).

If your husband is short-tempered and impatient, try remain-
ing silent in love. Stop participating in the vicious cycle of "he gets

angry; I get angry." Choose not to react during heated times. Wait until your husband has cooled down or is more rested before discussing things.

Suppose you had two dogs. Let's say one was red and the other blue. What would happen if you fed only the red dog and not the blue one? The red dog would become bigger and stronger while the blue one became weaker. Over time, Red would thrive, while Blue shriveled away.

Every time you act in a loving way toward your husband, it's as if you're feeding the red dog and refusing to feed the blue one. The basic principle is simple: *Feed Red, and starve Blue!* Each time you do this, it becomes more and more a part of your natural response. What you're doing is training your mind to think in a new way, and each successive attempt becomes easier.

Begin now to pray that you will have the strength to do this, and begin praying scripturally and fervently for your husband.

How to Pray Scripturally

An example is given in Colossians of a powerful way to pray. You might consider praying for your husband in such a way. Pray that he will

- be filled with the knowledge of God's will,
- have spiritual wisdom and understanding,
- walk in a manner worthy of the Lord, living a life full of integrity,
- please the Lord in all respects and do those things that bring glory to God,
- bear fruit in every good work,
- increase in the knowledge of God,

- be strengthened with all power according to the Lord's glorious might,
- attain steadfastness and patience,
- joyously give thanks to the Father, who has qualified us to share in the inheritance of the saints in the kingdom of light. (Colossians 1:9–12)

Pursuing Peaceful Relationships

For let [her] who wants to enjoy life and see good days (good whether apparent or not), keep [her] tongue free from evil, and [her] lips from guile (treachery, deceit)… Let [her] search for peace—harmony, undisturbedness from fears, agitating passions—moral conflicts—and seek it eagerly. —Do not merely desire peaceful relations [with God, with your fellowmen, and with yourself], *but pursue, go after them!* (1 Peter 3:10–11, AMP)

We are to actively pursue peaceful relations, not just desire them or wait on them to come our way. Many times our hurt or pride paralyzes us and prevents us from seeking peace with our husbands.

Not long after I (Nancy) had begun to study and apply God's Word to my marriage, I was given an opportunity to live what I was learning. Our daughter Anne had been looking for a vintage 1966 Mustang automobile. She and her dad eventually found the perfect car: yellow with black leather interior. Ray generously bought it for her and instructed her to watch the oil gauge since it was an older car and used oil more quickly. One day he got a call from Anne, who had just arrived at work.

"Dad, the car is acting strangely. I don't think it has any oil."

Ray was not pleased! We went to Anne's rescue, taking along our other daughter, Christine. As we drove, he verbalized his annoyance with Anne. Since I was completely innocent, I was quite unhappy to listen to what he really should have been telling her.

We arrived at her workplace, and Ray replenished the oil. As we were driving home, he continued to express his disbelief that this could have happened after all the warnings he gave her. I hadn't wanted to hear about it on the way over, and certainly I didn't want to hear about it again on the drive back! Yet what I had learned about pursuing peaceful relations with my husband was fresh in my mind. With great effort, I chose to remain quiet.

This was new to me! My old reaction would have been to utter a few choice words. Instead, I thought about what had just happened. My husband is a wonderful man. He had bought our daughter a beautiful car, and she had been careless with it. And instead of leaving her in the middle of a parking lot trying to figure out what to do, he came to her rescue willingly.

As we drove home, in the midst of his reprise of disbelief, I commented to him, "What a loving dad you are to help Anne when she didn't really deserve it." This comment mysteriously and completely defused him. He immediately returned to his pleasant self.

When we got home, our daughter Christine whispered to me, "Mom, how did you do that?"

"It was God's grace," I told her. She knew it was true because she knew how I usually reacted.

There is no limit to what can happen in a marriage when you begin to apply what you've learned. The blessings are showered down not only on you, but also on those around you. One of the sweetest is knowing that God is attentive to your prayers.

> The eyes of the Lord are upon the righteous…and His ears are attentive to their prayer. But the face of the Lord is against those who practice evil. (1 Peter 3:12, AMP)

It is almighty God Himself who will oppose, frustrate, and defeat the one who chooses ungodly ways.

Life is full of opportunities to live out what you profess to believe, and not only your children are watching you. God is observing you as well. As He focuses on you and your life, is He pleased? Are you honoring the Lord by the way you embrace your role as a wife?

CLASSIC BEAUTY

It is wonderful to realize that when we live God's way and through His power, something happens to us *inwardly* and *outwardly*:

> …our faces shining with the brightness of his face. And so we are transfigured much like the Messiah, our lives gradually becoming brighter and more beautiful as God enters our lives and we become like him. (2 Corinthians 3:18, *The Message*)

This is classic beauty in the timeless sense. No blushes, powders, creams, or lotions can give what is being talked about here. *It comes from God alone.* As we allow Him entry into our hearts, the royal paintbrush of His glory is stroked across our lives, and we find ourselves becoming more and more like Him. This is the only beauty that really matters.

Holy beauty.

Simply put, her makeup doesn't make a woman beautiful—her *Maker* does!

Part Four

Priorities

Chapter Eight: First Things First

My mother had the nerve to put me third. I asked her one day why she did things this way. She said first came God, then Daddy, then me. And that was the way He meant it to be. *I'm third,* I thought. Not liking the news, I decided to discuss it with my friend Lou.

"Third," gasped Lou, "what a horrible spot. I'm first in my home, and I like it a lot."

"What about God and your daddy?" asked innocent me.

"Well, I'm first—I'm not sure who's two and who's three. I don't know much about God, but I sure outrank Dad. All he seems to do is make Mama mad. So I'm her number one girl; that's what she calls me. I'd lots rather be one than dumb number three."

The years went by, and I nearly forgot that conversation. Until thirty years later, when I saw Lou again—oh, how I'd missed my dear childhood friend. "Do you remember our talk," Lou said to me, "about how your mom made you be number three?" My memory was fuzzy, but the impression was there. Lou looked at me longingly, then said with despair, "I'd give anything now to be number three. I've learned about life—that's the way it should be. My mother was wrong to put me number one. She just didn't know how it should have been done. Your foundation was sure; mine was shaky at best. I never quite know how I fit with the rest." Lou let out a sigh, then uttered the words, "What a privilege it was for you to be third."

I went back to my mother's lovely small home in the same little town, where she now lived alone. Daddy had died just three years ago. Oh, how we miss him, you'll never know. My mother looked up as I came through the door. I looked at her gently, then stared at the floor. "Mom…" I began, a small tear being shed. Then I told her about what Lou had just said.

My mother smiled softly and then said to me, "It wasn't my nerve that made you number three. It was my love—can you now understand? I was just carrying out God's almighty plan."

It was her love. Of course! Now I see! Her love for God, for Daddy, for *me!*

First Things First

It is a life-changing thing to allow
His priorities to become yours.

*Y*ears ago, in a city near my hometown, I (Connie) was sitting with my family in a store where milk was sold. The store was quite old and a landmark of sorts. In addition to selling milk, it had a delightful stainless steel soda fountain where you could order ice-cream cones, banana splits, sundaes, and other delights. The family budget was tight and allowed little room for extras, so ordering from the fountain was a special treat for all of us. We usually did this in the summers after swimming in a nearby lake.

Vinyl-covered booths lined one wall of the store to provide additional seating. By the door was an antique scale where you could weigh yourself. It was massive in size and seemed to me better suited for weighing heavy animals. The dial indicating your weight was so large that everyone in the store could see it from wherever they sat. My sisters and I couldn't wait to get on the scale and weigh, and my dad usually did as well. My mother, however, never shared our excitement. This was a mystery to me at the time, although now I fully understand her reticence!

"WHO DO YOU LOVE MOST?"

On this particular occasion, we had gotten our order and were seated at a booth. I suspect we had already weighed ourselves three or four times. I distinctly remember looking across the table into my father's clear blue eyes and asking him whether he loved my mother or my sisters and me the most. Without hesitating, he said he loved each of us with all of his heart, but then he went on to explain that my mother held a higher position than we did in his life. That, he believed, was the way God intended it to be. His first love was for God, then for my mother, then for us girls.

I turned to my mother and asked the same question. She replied as my father had. "I love you dearly," she said, "but Daddy comes ahead of you girls." Was I discouraged or hurt? Not at all. I remember smiling from ear to ear as I licked my butterscotch revel ice-cream cone; I loved their answers to my question. It felt great knowing that they held one another in such high esteem, and it gave me a tremendous sense of security knowing we children couldn't uproot or supplant their relationship.

My family was not the exception. Most of my friends' parents felt the same way. Children, though greatly loved, ranked below the parents' commitment to each other. That was just the way it was, and as far as any of us knew, the way it was supposed to be. How quickly things change, though, from one generation to another.

A GENERATION LATER

As we've talked to women about the relationships in their homes, one thing has stood out time and time again: Most women feel that apart from their relationship with God, their relationship with their children is the most important. Many know their husbands should outrank their children, but the majority said that when it came right down to it that's not the way it plays out.

As a result, the structure and hierarchy of family life has been turned topsy-turvy. Homes have become child-centered, and dads are often on the periphery looking in.

Not surprisingly, husbands often feel shunted aside and out of the loop. The marriage relationship is placed on the back burner, while the parenting relationship becomes all-consuming. Many women, feeling that they are the more gifted in parenting, frequently take the lead and relegate their husbands to the role of assistant.

PRIORITIES ARE IMPORTANT

When God formed Eve from the rib of Adam, His plan for the family was set in place. He created Eve to be a helpmate to Adam and relieve his aloneness. After this occurred, children were born into the family.

A wife's role is not meant to be abandoned or amended once children come along. Certainly it is expanded, but her commitment to her husband and her respect for his place in the family are to remain unchanged. Even though she is now a mother, she should still see herself as a helper to her husband.

God says that a man is to leave his father and mother and cleave to his wife (Genesis 2:24). A woman should not leave her husband—even in a psychological sense—and cleave to her children, yet that is what is happening in many modern households.

To do this injures you, your family, and your relationship with God.

Marriage is intended to be the highest form of love and communication that exists between two people. To replace this relationship with your relationship with your children is to alter God's plan for your life.

The Family Vacation

The family was excited. Summer vacation was upon them and they were ready to head out for the eight-hundred-mile trip to their favorite camp in Minnesota. As the last bag was thrown into the trunk of the car, chaos broke loose. All three children scurried to sit in the front seat beside the driver. After much arguing, Johnny, the oldest, declared that since his legs were the longest, he should sit up front.

Everyone loaded into the car according to the son's directions. Dad asked Mom if she wouldn't rather sit up front with him, but she insisted that she didn't mind the backseat at all, especially since this would please Johnny. His parents had dubbed him a natural leader early on, so the fact that his preferences prevailed was not unusual.

When Mom decided to take over for Dad at the wheel, Dad told Johnny to move into the backseat. Johnny turned to his mother and begged her to let him stay put. The pitiful look on his face was all Mom could see. As her firstborn, he had always held a special place in her heart, and it was difficult for her to deny his request.

Mom turned to Dad and said, "I sat in the backseat for three hundred miles. You can too." In disbelief, Dad said that he had done his share of backseat sitting when he was a boy and had no intentions of doing so as a forty-year-old man. His remarks were greeted by a deafening silence from Mom.

Dad once again told Johnny to get into the backseat. Mom, in a clipped tone, said that Johnny would not be comfortable in the backseat because his legs were so long. Dad reminded Mom that he was two inches taller than Johnny. Johnny and his brothers waited in anticipation, knowing what the outcome would be. Sure enough, a few minutes later Johnny was back up front and stayed there for the duration of the trip.

As Dad said later to a friend, "The real issue isn't who sits in the front seat. The real issue is that my wife consistently puts our children ahead of me, and in doing so, she negates any sense of authority I attempt to model within our home."

Such scenes play out in various ways across America today. Women have somehow convinced themselves that they are doing a noble thing by putting their children first. They seem to feel that this makes them better parents and will result in happier, more secure children. We believe that they are wrong. Women's priorities may have changed over the years, but God's have not.

A professor at a Christian college recently addressed this issue. He said that many parents today actually worship their children by unwittingly allowing them to be the authority in the home. In many Christian homes, he said, life often revolves around what pleases the children instead of what pleases God. So intent are parents on bonding with their children that they allow their marital relationship to flounder, and often their relationship with God is neglected as well.

The media-driven age in which we live tells us over and over again that the most important thing you can do for your children is to give them a strong self-image. While a healthy self-image is beneficial, even desirable, there is something that is far more foundational. It is teaching our children to love God.

> Love the LORD your God with all your heart and with all your soul and with all your strength. These command-ments that I give you today are to be upon your hearts. *Impress them on your children.* Talk about them when you sit at home and when you walk along the road, when you lie down and when you get up. Tie them as symbols on your hands and bind them on your foreheads. Write them on the doorframes of your houses and on your gates. (Deuteronomy 6:5–9)

We are to be teaching our children about God *all the time!* It's the most important thing that we can do for them. If children are taught this, their self-esteem is well on its way to being anchored securely.

How are the relationships in your life aligned? Where does the one with your husband rank? Your children? If more emphasis is placed on the latter, then you have fallen into the trap of placing your children first. This seems like a sweet thing to do, yet to do so denies your husband his rightful place in your life.

If you were to ask your husband, "Do you feel that I place you ahead of our children?" what would he say? I (Connie) once asked my husband this question.

"Are you serious?" he asked. "The answer seems so obvious. I'm surprised you would have to ask."

His answer didn't surprise me; I knew it was true. I had been raised by parents who had consistently put each other first, and I had loved the fact that they did. Yet somewhere along the road, I had failed to do this in my own marriage.

What makes a woman do this? Many times her husband is not meeting her needs like she feels he should, so she turns to her children in hopes that they will. Frequently she has become disenchanted in the marriage and refocuses her hopes and dreams on the lives of her children. Some women were raised in dysfunctional homes and are determined that their children will not experience the same upbringing that they did. Whatever the reason, if you sense that your priorities are out of order in your home, with God's help begin changing them now!

MOTHERING YOUR HUSBAND

I (Connie) once asked my husband the following question: "If you could choose one behavior for me to stop, what would it be?" I had begun to change in my marriage, and I was in a data-gathering mode.

His answer was immediate and to the point: "I'd want you to stop mothering me." He didn't have to think about it for a second. My mothering skills not only encompassed our children, but him too. Women often wonder where the romance has gone in their marriage. Yet as my husband explained to me, it is hard for a man to feel romantic toward a woman who is constantly mothering him, however well-intentioned her actions might be.

What might mothering one's husband look like? We asked a large group of women and men. Almost without fail, criticizing their husband's driving was near the top of the list. It's as if this is in a woman's DNA. Men, however, aren't interested in our helpful hints about how they can get somewhere faster, more safely, more scenically, or with less wear on the brakes. One woman told us that at one point this issue had become so touchy in her marriage that often she and her husband wouldn't be speaking to one another when they arrived at their destination. "Letting go of that was one of the smartest things I ever did," she told us. "We have so much more fun when we're out together. I no longer nitpick, and he no longer gets upset."

Another way of mothering your husband might be telling him how to dress. If he's under- or overdressed for an occasion, lovingly suggest that he consider something else, but don't insist on it. Allow him his own style—don't force your fashion preferences on him. Generally speaking, unless he asks your opinion, let him dress as he likes.

Don't chastise or cajole him about leaving his clothes lying around. Certainly this isn't to say that you can't respectfully ask him to put his clothes away, but avoid nagging him if he doesn't do so immediately.

Don't micromanage his diet, his exercise, or how he spends his free time. Also, don't take it upon yourself to change things in his life that only he can change—for example, smoking, cursing, or gambling. Again, there is nothing wrong with discussing behavior that concerns you, but do so in a respectful manner with the realization that it's not up to you to change your husband. Many times a wife's gentle, loving ways prompt change in her husband as much as anything else.

For many couples, money is an area where the wife is tempted to mother her husband. It is degrading and insulting to a man for his wife to "hover" over his spending habits. If there is a real problem in this area, seek godly counsel. However, if it is simply a difference of personal preferences, don't try to control or manipulate your husband into doing things your way.

Mothering your husband takes a multitude of forms, and we've mentioned only a few. You might be surprised to hear what your husband has to say about it. Consider asking his opinion. If he's feeling overly mothered, ask for practical suggestions on ways you could change. If he does express himself, don't become defensive.

One woman said, "I thought I could tend only to my husband or to my children. There wasn't time or energy to do both. It was obvious who needed me more, so I took care of my children and mentally placed my husband on autopilot. I figured that one day when the children were gone, I'd work him back into my life, so to speak. However, as I began to reprioritize my relationships, I discovered that he didn't need tending as a mother tends to a child. What he needed was a wife. *And my children needed a mother who put their father first.*

"Years later one of my daughters was struggling with this same issue in her life. 'Mom, the best thing you ever did for me was to honor Dad like you did. So many days I find myself deferring to the children and shortchanging my husband. When this happens I think of your example, and this helps me get back on track.' I hadn't always been a mother who did this, but thankfully, this is what my daughter remembers."

The effects of prioritizing relationships are far-reaching. Not only does it influence your relationship with God and your husband, but it influences the kind of spouse your daughter will be or the kind of woman your son may choose for his wife. God has given us the privilege of modeling priorities that not only honor

Him and our husbands, but also influence our children to honor God more fully in their own marriages.

THREE YEARS OR THIRTY?

Not long ago we were at a local restaurant. The family seated nearby included a three-year-old girl, her parents, and her grandparents. Even as they were seated, we noticed that the little girl seemed to call the shots. She insisted on being seated in a high chair even though the rest of the group preferred that she sit in a booster seat. She then demanded that her two stuffed animals, which she had brought with her, be allowed to sit in their own high chairs. Many people in the restaurant sat and watched as chairs were rearranged to make room. The little girl was the queen bee, and she had two members in her adoring audience: her mother and grandmother. The men sat silently at the far end of the table, staring at the menus.

Every word the little girl spoke caused the women to beam, but the men didn't seem to share their enthusiasm. Rarely did they speak, except to give an occasional answer to a direct question. About twenty minutes later, a couple that had been seated near this group got up to leave. They stopped at the three high chairs and said something to the little girl. Then they turned to the adults and said, "She certainly commands all of the attention, doesn't she?"

"That's been going on for three years now," the little girl's father agreed.

"Three years?" the grandfather suddenly piped up. "It's been going on for a lot longer than that. Try thirty years," he said, indicating that this very thing had happened with this child's mother, his daughter. This remark was followed by awkward laughter as the couple left, at which point the men went back to eating their dinner and the women went back to watching the child, their suppers untouched.

WHEN GOD'S DESIGN IS ALTERED

Rearranging God's design for the family affects not only this generation, but also those to come. Proverbs 22:6 tells us to "train a child in the way he should go, and when he is old he will not turn from it." If you are putting your children ahead of their father, you are training them in error. Home is the school that matters most. What our children learn at home is what they will take with them when they marry and have families of their own. We often think of "training" our children as a verbal thing. What do we tell them? What can we say to make them understand a principle? However, "training our children" has as much to do with our actions as it does with our words. If we are telling them one thing but living out something else, they are receiving conflicting messages about God's Word, our convictions, and what it is we are teaching them.

THE EFFECTS ON CHILDREN

When a woman holds her children in higher regard than she does her husband, she is giving them an exaggerated sense of their own self-worth. They come to believe that they are more important than Dad and frequently see themselves as more important than others.

Remember Johnny, who rode in the front seat all the way to Minnesota? After leaving Minnesota, the family veered off course to visit Johnny's grandparents. The first morning there, Johnny came downstairs for breakfast. Two of the chairs at the table had comfortable pads, but the others did not. Johnny's grandfather was sitting in one of the padded chairs, so Johnny sat in the other. The rest of the family was still asleep. After getting the food on the table, Johnny's grandmother went to sit down and noticed that Johnny was sitting in her chair.

"Johnny," Grandmother said, "you're sitting in my chair. Would you mind if I sat there?"

"I want to sit here, Grandma," Johnny said. "The others are hard."

Both grandparents' eyes widened. After a word from his grandfather, Johnny grudgingly moved.

Placing your children first seems like such a sweet thing to do, yet to do this denies your husband his rightful place in your life.

The same thing occurred at his uncle's house. Johnny walked into the living room and settled comfortably into the rocking chair. "Johnny, that is the rocker Grandpa always sits in," Johnny's uncle said. Johnny retorted that he'd sat in the chair first, then stomped from the room, leaving his embarrassed parents to cover the awkward pause that ensued.

Johnny had not been taught to respect his elders or to defer to those in authority over him. He was acting in the only way he knew and in the manner that he regularly saw modeled in his home—that priority should be given to him. Whether Johnny is a natural born leader, as his parents think, remains to be seen. The issue isn't whether our children are natural born leaders, but whether they love and obey God. God help the family, business, or country led by a self-centered natural born leader!

Certainly we are not saying that you shouldn't adore your children. We adore ours. We're saying that because we love them so much we teach them about God's hierarchy and where they fit. God's love for them is just as great as it is for anyone else, but His plan includes respecting their elders and submitting to those in authority over them.

When you place your children first, you are treating your husband's position with disrespect and apathy, and you may well be teaching your children to treat him in the same manner. One woman told us that this occurred in her house for a number of years. She couldn't figure out why her children didn't have more respect for their father, because he tried so hard to be a good father to them.

"When I looked at myself and my priorities, I realized that I was the problem. By continually allowing the children's wants to take precedence over my husband's, I believe I was actually saying to them that their father's place, his opinions and preferences, were secondary to their own. I gave him no credibility, so why should they? When I began treating him as the head of our home and backing my words up with actions, our children began respecting him as well."

Most children feel that their fathers are supposed to be the heads of their homes, but few will grant them this position unless their parents model it first. When parents are living in harmony within the home, it gives children a sense of peace and security that nothing can replace.

GROWN CHILDREN

Even after children are grown, women often continue placing them ahead of their husbands. Adult children, especially daughters, can be extremely nurturing and warm toward their mothers. Don't let this draw you away from your husband or tempt you to give your child more regard than you do him. This is not to say that you shouldn't enjoy or receive the attention given you by your adult children. Certainly this is a wonderful thing. But it is a reminder not to let this alter your husband's position in your heart and home.

If a woman is unhappy in her marriage, she will often turn to a son or daughter to provide her with the companionship she is not receiving from her spouse. It's not unusual to see women grieve when their children leave for college or get married. Part of this grief is natural and comes from closing a chapter in the child's life. Many times, though, much of the grief comes because a woman made an unhealthy choice to have children fill the emotional needs that her husband was meant to fill.

HOW OUR HUSBANDS FEEL

How does it make a man feel when his wife puts their children ahead of him? We posed that question to a group of men. Their most common answers are listed below.

1. Insignificant and disrespected
Most replied that they felt a deep lack of respect from not only their wives, but from their children as well. "Respect is important to a man, and he doesn't feel that when the children consistently come first," said one man.

2. Unloved
Most men, unlike most women, associate love with actions instead of with feelings. When a woman places her children above her hus-

band, her actions say to him that she loves the children more than she loves him. Though not as vocal about it as women, men desire to be deeply loved by their wives. It is difficult for a man to see his wife cherish the children, but treat him in a cool or casual manner.

3. Lonely

One of man's greatest needs is companionship, and he usually expects to find this in his relationship with his wife. "As my wife pours more and more of her life into being a mother, she pours less and less of it into being my wife," said one man. "The friend I once had in my wife is now a friend to our children, but a stranger to me." The lonelier a man becomes, the more vulnerable he is to outside temptation. Is your husband lonely because of the time you spend with your children? Are you in any way making him more vulnerable to the attentions of other women?

4. Unappreciated

Men appreciate being appreciated! Many men feel that their wives show greater appreciation to their children than they do to them. "If our daughter goes to a friend's for the night, my wife misses her terribly," said one husband. "When she comes home the next morning, my wife is ecstatic to see her and acts as if she's been gone forever. I can be gone for days on a business trip, and my wife acts like I never left. Sometimes she even seems to resent my return home." Does your husband know how important he is to you and how much you value him? Are you an appreciative wife?

5. Resentful and Angry

Though not a majority, some men stated that when their wives put their children first, they felt a sense of resentment and anger; some felt this way toward their children, others toward their wives. "My fifteen-year-old son walks through the door, and my wife immediately asks about his day or rubs his back if he's tired. She pampers him constantly. I find myself resenting him, even though I know it isn't his fault." Is your husband frustrated or even jealous of your relationship with your children? Could it be that he feels left out or overlooked?

IDEAS TO CONSIDER

Maybe you're sensing that you need a major overhaul in this area, or perhaps just some fine-tuning. Regardless, here are some ideas to consider:

1. *Think positive thoughts.*
For every positive thought you have of your children, think of two for your husband. Begin noticing the many things he does. Perhaps he sees to it that the house is locked up every night or helps you replace lightbulbs. Men enjoy praise!

2. *Give him the benefit of the doubt.*
Often this comes easily with our children, but is more difficult with our husbands. Grant him the same gracious generosity that you so readily give your kids.

3. *Be spontaneous.*
Surprise him once a week with a random act of kindness. One woman recently discovered that her husband liked a slushy drink from a local convenience store. She began buying them for him. "He loves it when I do this. It's such a simple thing to do, and it lets him know I'm thinking about him."

4. Invest in his stock.

Share with your children things you admire about their father. This lets them see how important your marriage is to you. Though it's been said dozens of times, the way Mom sees Dad is the greatest influencer of how the children see him. Do this with others as well. Many women excel at communicating their children's strengths, but not their husband's. One woman pointed out that often friends will talk about their children in glowing terms, but when they talk about their husbands, they tend to talk about their weaknesses and inabilities. If you do this, stop! Commit to sharing with others only those things that build your husband up. Words are infectious and should be chosen wisely.

5. Make your bedroom a haven.

Too often this is the catchall room. Make an effort to keep it clean, organized, and inviting. One woman bought a small love seat and placed it in the master bedroom. This is where she and her husband spend a few moments together once they've gotten in the door at the end of the day. It shows their children that they value each other's company as well. Burn a fragrant candle so that the room smells inviting and warm.

6. Cater to his quirks.

Many times we think our children's quirks are cute but our husband's are obnoxious. One woman discovered that her husband liked his sheets changed often, yet she preferred going longer between changings. "I fought this for years," she said. "I thought he was being too obsessive. One day my daughter asked why I ignored her father's request for clean sheets but always changed hers whenever she asked. I was shocked. I didn't realize I did this.

I suddenly saw that I was not only dismissing one of my husband's rare requests, but I was also modeling wrong priorities for my daughter."

7. *Check your attitude.*
Said one woman, "I was stunned one night when my husband told me that he wished I had the same attitude toward him that I had toward the kids. From his perspective, I bent over backward for them. I ran all over town to find my daughter the right dress or my son the right tennis shoes. But he said that if he asked me to stop at the hardware store and pick up a gallon of paint, I balked." Our attitudes speak volumes to our husbands.

8. *Pray for your husband.*
This tip could go in every chapter. There is nothing like prayer to soften your heart and sharpen your focus.

9. *Reintroduce pet names into your relationship.*
Refrain from calling him "Dad" or "Daddy." Choose instead to call him by a name that shows your love and high regard for him as a husband.

Your husband may or may not respond as you reprioritize your relationships. It really isn't an issue, though, if you are doing it to honor God. Certainly it's nice for him to notice and appreciate your efforts, but it isn't necessary. God notices.

REFLECTIONS ON PROVERBS 31

There was a time in my (Connie) life when I struggled with this problem. My children were my top priority, and most of my energy went toward them. My husband, aware of how I felt, said little. Whenever the topic was discussed, I strongly defended the position I had taken. What could he say? I countered everything he brought up with my intention to give our children the best foundation possible. How could he argue with that?

In the midst of this, I sat down one morning to spend some time with the Lord. My Bible fell open to Proverbs 31.

Interesting, I thought to myself. *I'll read through these verses and then go on to something else.*

I began at verse 10: "A wife of noble character who can find? She is worth far more than rubies." I agreed totally. But verses 11 and 12 stopped me cold: "Her husband has full confidence in her and lacks nothing of value. She brings him good, not harm, all the days of her life."

My heart was stirred as I read those words, and I felt the Lord asking me, "Connie, does your husband have full confidence in you? Does he lack anything of value? Do you bring him good and not harm all the days of your life?"

I attempted to justify myself before Him, but of course it didn't work. He knows the innermost parts of my heart, and certainly He knew the truth.

"No, Lord," I finally answered, "my husband doesn't have full confidence in me. Sure, he has confidence that I won't leave him for another man, or treat our children badly, or do something that is totally off-the-wall. But he doesn't have full confidence that when I say he's the head of our home, I mean it. Or that I will defer to his leadership when we disagree on something. He doesn't have full confidence in knowing that he falls right under You on my priority list, for he's not an idiot, Lord. He wouldn't delude himself into thinking he ranked second to You. Or third. Or fourth. No, Lord, my husband doesn't have full confidence in me."

"Does your husband lack nothing of value?"

"No, Lord, I cannot say that he does. Yes, I keep his shirts clean and his underwear drawer full, and I even put gas in his car for him. But I know, Lord, that these aren't the kinds of things You're talking about. I know that the things spoken of here aren't things you hang on a hanger, place in a drawer, or purchase at the gas station. No, I think You're talking about things like his feeling loved no matter what kind of day I've had or mood I'm in. Things like knowing he has my unwavering loyalty and that I'll be by his side, no matter what life throws at him. He knows I'd be by his side, Lord, but he might wonder whether it was out of duty or devotion. If he lacked nothing of value, he'd never have to wonder about that for a second.

"Does he lack something of value, Lord? Yes, Lord, he does. He lacks knowing I'll forgive quickly. He lacks knowing I won't pick a fight the minute he walks through the door if I'm irritable or upset. He lacks knowing that I care deeply about him because I get too busy and distracted to do that sometimes. He lacks knowing that impatient words will be a rarity in our home. He lacks knowing that his wife is no longer a scorekeeper. He lacks knowing that she no longer monitors his responses. Does he lack any of these things, Lord? Yes, Lord, *some days he lacks them all.*"

Once again, the Lord probed my heart. "Do you bring him good, not harm, all the days of your life?" Jesus asked. "Does it bring him harm when he feels alone? Or when he feels battered by the world, but can't talk to you because you're too busy…too tired…too distracted…too caught up with the children? Does it bring him harm when he sees you taking care of everyone else in your life except him? Or when he's trying to pray, yet things aren't right between the two of you because of your stubbornness? Does it bring him harm when you constantly correct him over the most insignificant things? Or when you are a better mother to him than you are a wife?"

"Do I bring my husband good and not harm all the days of my life, Lord? No, I don't, Lord. *Not even close.*"

I was struck by the paradox that though I didn't do those things for my husband, I easily did them for my children.

My children have full confidence in me. They know I make mistakes or forget things from time to time, but by and large they know they can count on me 100 percent.

My children lack nothing of value. As much as possible, I make sure of that. Though not overly indulged materially, their physical, emotional, and spiritual needs are of the utmost importance to me, and I gladly attempt to make sure they are met. Yet I don't hold my husband's needs in the same regard. Or with the same urgency. *Or with the same joy.*

I attempt to bring my children good, not harm, all the days of my life. This is as natural as breathing for me as a mother, but not nearly as natural as a wife. There is nothing I wouldn't do for my kids. Yet I don't always do these things as eagerly for my husband, things such as taking his suitcase downstairs and putting it away. *You see, I was the woman in the story at the beginning of the book.*

I asked the Lord and my husband for forgiveness. I purposed to remember that this passage of Scripture is about a *godly wife,* not a godly mother. And from that day forward, I committed to prioritizing my relationships in a God-honoring way.

ONE FUTURE DAY

One day your children will look back over their lives and reflect on the people and events that helped mold them into who they are and what they believe. What will they see when they look at you? Will they see a mother who knew God's order for her life? Will they see a woman who took pleasure in being a godly wife? Or will they see a woman who chafed and resisted God's role for her in her marriage? Will you stand before them as a mother who taught them to respect their father because you respected him yourself? Or will they see a woman who treated her children with more dignity and love than she did her husband?

It is life-changing to allow His priorities to become your priorities. Will you do this? Will you line up your relationships His way? By doing so, you become more usable to Him, and the plain, earthenware jug of your life becomes a vessel of honor that brings glory to God.

May you become a priority specialist!

For your husband…

    For your children…

        For future generations to come…

            But most of all, for the kingdom of God!

Part Five

THE.
Motive

Chapter Nine: Why Am I Doing This?

Larry Crabb states, "The natural resistance to truly give ourselves to the other is rooted in our stubborn fear that if we really give, with no manipulative purpose, we will be shortchanged. Our needs will not be met. At best we'll be disappointed; at worst we'll be destroyed.

But God is faithful. We are to trust His perfect love to cast out our fear, believing that as we give to our spouse in His name, He will supernaturally bless us with an awareness of His presence. And He will. But it may take time—perhaps even months—before we sense His work in us. The willingness to give unconditionally does not come by simply deciding to be selfless. The stain of self-centeredness requires many washings before it no longer controls our motivation. Many commitments to minister and much time spent with God will transpire before we know what it means to give. Our job is to learn faithfulness and to press on in obedience, not giving in to discouragement or weariness, believing that God will always honor the conscious and persevering motivation to serve Him. When a spouse becomes critical, drinks more heavily, or rejects efforts of ministry, we are to continue in our obedience, believing that our responsibility before God is to obey and to trust Him for the outcome."[1]

Marriage…created to be a ministry. Is yours?

Why Am I Doing This?

It is an amazing thing to realize that as a woman serves her husband, Jesus Christ considers Himself the One served.

It was six o'clock in the morning, and I (Connie) was nearing the end of my run on the treadmill. I go regularly to my husband's place of employment and work out in the exercise room. A young woman I had never seen before came into the room, acknowledged me, and began walking on the treadmill beside me. She briefly looked over some note cards and then tossed them to the floor.

"Are you studying for something?" I asked.

"Yes," she replied, "I have boards coming up soon, and I'm trying to prepare for them."

After talking with her for a few minutes, I discovered that she was a fifth-year surgical resident and was six months away from completing the program. Written boards would follow, and she was beginning to review for them. She already had a job lined up in a nearby city.

She went on to say that she had just turned forty and had been married for five years. I asked her whether she thought her marriage was easier or harder than most, given the fact that she had waited until she was thirty-five to marry.

"You'd think it would be easier," she said, "but I'm not so sure. Marriage is hard. *Hard!* Far harder than medical school and residency combined."

Her bold statement piqued my interest, and I loved that she was so open and honest. "A friend and I are writing a book on marriage," I said, "so I find your comments fascinating. What do you think makes it so hard?"

"Do I have to be more specific than simply to say everything?" She laughed before going on. "I guess I would say that the most difficult thing is how marriage seems to boil down to two people reacting to one another. We didn't react when we were dating, yet now these reactions seem to define our marriage.

"Well," she continued, "I guess we did react when we were dating, but the reactions were positive. We were drawn to one another through them. But after the wedding, the reactions took a turn. Suddenly it's one negative reaction after another, and instead of being drawn together we've drifted apart."

I asked for an example.

"Say my husband hurts my feelings. I express that my feelings are hurt and attempt to tell him why. He becomes defensive and says I'm too sensitive. I question his ability to gauge my sensitivity level and suggest he look into a course on sensitivity training. He responds with a remark of his own. Before you know it, we're not speaking to one another, and neither of us can even remember the original problem."

"What gets you back on track?" I asked.

"Usually, after a day or two, both of us grow weary of this

behavior, and we begin to slowly treat one another with civility again. However, I can't help but believe that every time we do this, we get further and further from the marriage we had both hoped for because now, even when things are good, they're not all that great." She sighed and shook her head.

Her honesty and vulnerability surprised me. Here was a woman who would seem to have the world at her feet. She was attractive, intelligent, and pleasant. Very soon a successful medical practice would be hers as well. Yet here she was, at six in the morning, talking with a stranger about the pitfalls of marriage.

I then asked a penetrating question that had served as one of the turning points in my own marriage: "What is your motive for being married?"

A puzzled look crossed her face. "Motive? What a strange question." With a chuckle she said, "I think of *murder* and *motive* going together, not *marriage* and *motive*. Let's see, what is my motive? Surely if I can get through a surgical residency, I can come up with a plausible-sounding motive for marriage—but I can't."

She thought for a few moments more, but remained stumped. She had no idea what her motive for marriage was. *Do you?*

MOTIVES

For years we were like the woman in the story. We had no idea that God had something to say about motive in marriage. One of us did not know the Lord, and although the other did, there was complete ignorance in this regard. We wanted to be happy in our marriages and hoped our husbands were as well, but frequently this was not the case. Once we began learning our job descriptions as wives, we quickly discovered that unless a woman's motive for her marriage lines up with God's plan, fulfillment and satisfaction will elude her.

The apostle Paul, inspired by the Holy Spirit, told us what God said about motives:

> Whatever you do, work at it with all your heart, as working for the Lord, not for men, since you know that you will receive an inheritance from the Lord as a reward. It is the Lord Christ you are serving. (Colossians 3:23–24)

Do you see it? "It is the *Lord Christ* you are serving." That's the motive for your marriage. As you serve your husband, you are actually serving *Him*. What an incredible opportunity!

Too often we think of marriage as a relationship between two people. More than that, though, it is about our relationship with the Lord. Perhaps this is news to you. Is it good news or bad?

Satan attempts to make you focus on yourself and what you want, as he did with Eve in the Garden. Doing this causes you to forget the "as unto the Lord" part of your marriage.

This passage is the nuts and bolts not only of marriage, *but also of life itself.* It illustrates a simple but powerful process, and when you choose to implement it in your marriage, you will never be the same.

WORK AT IT WITH ALL YOUR HEART

Whatever you do, you are to work at it with all your heart: cleaning the house, wiping a nose, visiting a neighbor, carrying out job responsibilities, serving in church, *being a wife.*

When you work without putting your heart into it, the outcome is compromised and the process is stagnating and unfulfilling.

When I (Connie) was a young girl, my parents went to town one morning to buy groceries. They told my sister and me to go out to the garden and pick the green beans while they were gone. It was summertime, and we wanted to watch a few programs on television that we didn't normally get to see. This sounded far more fun than working in the garden. After a brief consultation, we decided that we would blitz the rows of beans, picking just enough to appease our parents. We grabbed two small sacks and filled them. We set the beans on the back porch, headed to our black-and-white television set, and eagerly turned it on. Ah, the rewards of a hard morning's work!

A few hours later our parents came home and asked if we had done our chores.

"Yes," we replied, I suspect a bit anxiously. We mentally crossed our fingers and hoped that would be the end of it.

"Where are the beans you picked?" my mother asked. "I think I'll snap some for supper."

"On the back porch," I answered, suddenly wishing I had done a better job.

We heard the back door open and exchanged nervous glances as our mother went out. We then heard Mom conferring with Dad. He called us to the back porch, and, hearts dropping, we went.

"I thought you said you picked the beans," Dad said.

"Well, we kind of did," we said, trying our best to sound convincing.

"'Kind of' isn't good enough. When you've been given a job to do, you do it the best way you know how. I don't want to hear any more about this 'kind of' stuff. Now, go get a couple of sacks and let's go pick the beans."

Is that how you're living—in a "kind of" fashion? Can you see that if that's what you're doing, you're serving the Lord in that same manner? Don't you want to be a woman who serves Him with excellence? One way you can do this is by ministering to your husband. When you do, your motive and God's Word are aligned, and that is where deep satisfaction and peace lie.

"TELL ME MORE"

One morning while we were working on this book, a friend called. She asked how the writing was going. We told her we were in the middle of this chapter. "It's about the whole idea of marriage being a ministry," we told her.

"Fascinating concept," she said, enunciating the words as only someone from England can. "I like that thought, although frankly, I must say that I have no idea what you mean by ministry. You see, I was raised in a church that didn't speak about ministry, so I'm a bit confused by the whole thing. I'd love to know more, though."

Ministry simply means "to serve." When a pastor comes to minister to a church, he comes to serve the people and the needs in that church. Ultimately, though, he is serving God.

That is what is meant by ministry in your marriage. As a wife, you are to minister to, or serve, your husband. As you do so, Jesus considers Himself served.

Marriage as a ministry was a life-changing concept for us and totally revolutionized the way we interacted with and served our husbands. Jesus Christ was now a part of the picture. Certainly we already knew He was in our midst, but when we realized that the way we treated our husbands was considered by Jesus to be the way we treated Him, it forced us to take a hard look at our actions in our marriages.

BEGINNING TO CHANGE

Once you understand this concept, you can begin to see how the idea of ministry in marriage might bring changes to your life.

Let's say your husband has told you he'll be home at five-thirty in the evening and will be ready for dinner at six. Uncharacteristically, he's not home, and it's now six o'clock. The meal is ready, and the children (and you!) are growing hungrier by the minute.

Six-thirty comes and goes and still no husband. You decide to go ahead and feed the children and are cleaning up after them at seven o'clock when your husband comes through the door. Normally, your first reaction might be, "Where were you? Why didn't you call? You're an hour late and dinner is cold." You want to let him know the inconvenience and irritation he's caused you.

However, if you view marriage as a ministry, your first thought would be for him. You would cheerfully greet him and ask if everything was okay. You would tell him how glad you are that he's home and graciously reheat his dinner. You might offer him compassion and warmth, letting him know how sorry you are that his day was so long. Certainly it's fine

More often than not, pride is what chokes out a ministering spirit in a marriage.

to ask him later on to please call the next time he's running late, but guard against doing so in an exasperated, judgmental fashion.

Are you beginning to get the picture? Or does it seem rather one-sided to you? Could pride be rearing its ugly head? More often than not, pride is what chokes out a ministering spirit in a marriage. Did you know that God actually resists the proud? Proverbs 3:34 says that God resists the proud but gives grace to the humble.

I (Connie) have wrestled with pride in my marriage many times. When this occurs, ministering to my husband is the last thing I feel like doing. I know what I'm called to do—but I don't want to do it.

Why would God bless an attitude like that? Be assured, He wouldn't! No wonder I feel so miserable when those times occur. I'm not only missing out on God's blessing; I am experiencing His *resistance* as well.

As you begin to minister to your husband "as unto the Lord," you may need to remind yourself, especially at first, why you are choosing to do this: You're actually serving Jesus when you serve your husband.

Our model is Christ Himself:

But whosoever will be great among you let him be your minister; And whosoever will be chief among you let him be your servant; Even as the Son of man came not to be ministered unto, but to minister and to give his life a ransom for many. (Matthew 20:26–28, KJV)

Isn't it tempting to think only about wanting to be ministered to? Yet Jesus set the example for ministry: It is to be *others focused*. Once again you might be tempted to think that your ministry to your husband depends on him doing his part. So many times women tell us that things like this will work only if he does his part and that it has to be mutual. But this simply isn't true. Your husband might *never* do his part. Does that give you permission to disobey Jesus' command? Of course not! Why would you allow someone else's ungodly choice to impact your own? How many times have you told your children to do what they know to be right, even if they're the only ones doing it? The same is true for you!

As you live this way, you will see seemingly trivial things in your life begin to change. Ministering will create great inroads to joy and peace into your marriage. I (Nancy) remember how this occurred in my marriage. This took place almost twenty years ago, yet it still comes vividly to mind.

WHO WILL WALK THE DOG?

I had been a Christian for a short time when I heard a speaker who encouraged us to have prayer time every morning. She suggested that we pray for one hour. I thought to myself, *An hour? How can a person pray that long?* But I wanted to try.

About the same time, a friend asked me, "What does your husband do for you?"

I thought. And thought. And thought some more. Never mind that I was able to stay home, had a new car, and lived in a lovely home. My husband was a wonderful man, and I had a great life, yet I could think of nothing. I finally said, "He walks our dog." My husband had given me a dog for Christmas, and he walked him every morning.

I awoke for my prayer time that first morning and slipped out of bed. I quietly left the room and closed the door behind me. The dog began to bark and scratch at the door. My husband called out, "Where are you?" I replied, "I'm praying." So he got out of bed and dutifully took care of the dog.

The next day, the same thing happened. My husband asked, "What are you doing?"

"I'm *praying*," I said, this time a little more emphatically.

"For the whole world?" he asked in frustration. Again, he got out of bed and took care of the dog.

On the third day I awoke and started to slip out of the room. Once again the dog began to scratch the door and bark to be taken outside. I thought to myself, *What is the big deal here? I'll walk the dog before praying.*

A bit grudgingly, I took the dog outside. I still remember the beauty of that early morning. The sky was magnificent, and the moon cast shadows about me. I'm not sure I had ever seen the stars in the early morning. The birds were chirping. It was a new day, and I was so thankful to be a part of it. The cool air stirred my soul. As I walked to the end of the driveway, I noticed the newspaper lying there.

I thought, "Why don't I take him the newspaper, along with a cup of coffee?" So I did. This seemingly insignificant choice was the beginning of my developing a new heart of love for my husband and receiving an overwhelming supply of love from him. I had chosen to serve him. In doing so, I had chosen to serve the Lord as well.

I felt so happy. Joy and contentment flooded my soul. I knew without a doubt that I was in a place of blessing from the Lord.

Had I not chosen to walk the dog, I never would have experienced the beauty of the morning or noticed the newspaper lying in the driveway. I wouldn't have picked it up or thought about taking my husband a cup of coffee.

Who would have thought that such a small, seemingly inconsequential thing would change my marriage so radically? Yet it did, because it began the change in me.

CHANGE STARTS WITH YOU

Is your marriage in need of change? Perhaps it has been so cold for so long that it seems hopelessly frozen. But it's not! Can you begin to see that, regardless of how you've conducted yourself in your marriage before, it's time to conduct yourself "as unto the Lord"?

Perhaps this is disheartening news to you. You may not be ready to treat your husband in this manner, yet you can no longer justify your current treatment of him. What are you called to do in such a case? You are called to be obedient to God's Word, regardless of your feelings toward your husband.

No doubt, your husband has made mistakes many times. Perhaps he has hurt your feelings, made an error in judgment, or been unduly harsh with you or the children. When this happens, it's natural to feel that he doesn't deserve to be treated well. Your tendency might be to withdraw or lash out at him.

But the real issue isn't how your husband deserves to be treated, *but how Jesus deserves to be treated.* This makes it so simple! And it is motivating as well.

When you treat your husband coldly, it's as if Jesus Christ is right there with you, and you're treating Him coldly too. This puts things in a completely different perspective. The way you're serving Christ right now—today—is a direct reflection of the way you're serving your husband. In fact, it's been said that your present relationship with your husband is a spiritual barometer of your relationship with Christ. The Lord notices your efforts and promises a reward for your faithful service.

An Inheritance from the Lord

One of God's great promises is that He will reward you for the work you do as a sincere expression of your devotion to Him. *He notices what you do!* Don't look to your husband to reward you for your ministry to him. God will do this!

There is a present reward—you will experience His presence and His power through the Holy Spirit. The supernatural outcome of this is fruit bearing.

And there is a future reward as well. There will be a time in eternity when Christ will reward you. He will give you crowns:

- A crown that lasts forever. (1 Corinthians 9:25)
- A crown of exultation. (1 Thessalonians 2:19, NASB)
- A crown of righteousness. (2 Timothy 4:8)
- The Chief Shepherd's crown of glory. (1 Peter 5:4)
- A crown of gold. (Revelation 4:4)

How wonderful to have crowns to lay at His nail-pierced feet. What else would we have to give Him? After all, we have nothing to boast of as we serve Him because anything done for Him is enabled *by* Him.

Ministering to a Difficult Husband

Perhaps your husband is distant toward you and you are battling resignation and discouragement. Perhaps your husband is outright cold or mean-spirited or frequently puts you down. It is especially important for you to serve your husband "as unto the Lord" during those times and not slip back into believing that your husband's response determines your actions. It is helpful to remember that your will, not your feelings, determines your actions. This doesn't mean your feelings of hurt or rejection will automatically disappear—they won't. It means that you are choosing to serve God regardless of your husband's behavior. Fervently seek God during those times and ask Him to heal your wounds.

We know of a woman whose husband constantly blamed her for their poor marriage, even though it appeared she was working at it with all her heart. What did she do? She prayed even more fervently for her husband and her marriage and asked God to give her the strength to serve her husband as she would Him. And she boldly asked Him to enable her to do it in a joyful manner. "My hope is that my marriage will eventually change. But my greater hope is that I can one day stand before the Lord and have Him say to me, 'Well done, good and faithful servant. You were faithful to the end.'"

It's easy to lose focus. This is especially true if you have a husband who is not responding to your efforts. God knows what is happening. Although at times He may seem far away, He is not. He is right there, closer than the beat of your heart, waiting to comfort and encourage you. He sees every action, hears every word, notes every hurt. He sees you pushing on as the storm rages around you, *and He does not forget it.* Scripture assures us of that.

This may be all you have to hold on to. Remember that your heavenly Father will one day look at you and reward you for your godly behavior. Your heartache and pain will be erased forever, and you will receive an inheritance like no other—a royal inheritance given to you personally by Jesus Christ.

Does your motive need to change? Doing so is just a choice away.

THE HUSBAND PARAPHRASE

We thought it would be fitting to end this chapter with our paraphrase of Matthew 25:35–40.

> *I was hungry for breakfast, dinner,*
> *and sometimes even lunch, snacks,*
> *a kind word, a warm hug, to talk to you, to be loved by you....*
> *You gave me something to eat.*
> *I was thirsty to feel accepted by you,*
> *to take the leadership role in our home,*
> *to be admired by you, to be respected by you.*
> *I mowed the lawn and needed refreshing and....*
> *You gave me something to drink.*
> *I was a stranger; my mood was bad.*
> *I had been unreasonable.*
> *I had been mean, thoughtless, forgetful, unhelpful, self-centered....*
> *You invited me in.*
> *I was naked, you did all my wash*
> *even when I dropped it on the floor.*
> *You sewed on my missing buttons.*
> *You ironed my wrinkled shirts.*
> *You let me bare my soul to you.*
> *You saw the real me that others never see—*
> *with all my quirks and uncovered ugliness,*

and you never exposed me before our children, family, or friends....
You clothed me.
I was sick—you know my colds are worse than anyone else's.
Sometimes I said things to you I didn't mean.
I got depressed and.... You cared for me.
I was in prison: my job got to me some days and I withdrew from you.
When I was lonely you were there for me.
You prayed for me.
When I was consumed with a problem,
when I was unforgiving, when I didn't deserve anything
because of the way I've treated you and I was so ashamed....
You came to me.
Jesus would say to you, "When you did these things for
your husband, you did them for Me."

Press on! An inheritance from the Lord awaits you.

Press on! Can't you hear the trumpets sounding? The heavens applauding? Can't you imagine the misting of your eyes as they meet the sweet soft gaze of His? Can't you sense the swelling of your heart and the joyful singing of your soul as He wraps His loving arms around you and says, "Well done"?

Press on! As you serve your husband, you serve the King of kings and Lord of lords! Your efforts are of great worth to Him!

Part Six

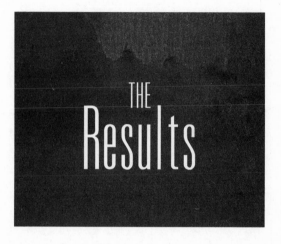

THE
Results

Chapter Ten: A Speechless Husband Speaks

What could be worse than never to be first in the heart of your precious bride?

What could be harder than to have a son or daughter take your place and push you aside?

What could be dearer than to be loved and nearer your wife than all others combined?

A Speechless
Husband Speaks

*How very blessed is the man who has
a wife who walks with God.*

*While in the midst of writing this book, we were privileged to hear a
husband give testimony of how his wife's desire to honor God in their
marriage profoundly impacted his own life. We thought you'd enjoy it
as well. As you'll see from his words, when a woman chooses to honor
God in the way she treats her husband, the outcome could be that far
more lives are changed than simply her own.*

I feel fortunate to write of God's great work in our marriage. The principles taught in this book have changed
my wife, our marriage, and my life almost beyond belief.
I tend to be a perfectionist, and as a newlywed I had a certain
idea of what marriage should be like. My expectations were high—
for myself, for the marriage, and certainly for my wife. She was a

great spouse who did her best to make our marriage good, but my expectations were so high that in my eyes she often fell short. Coupled with this, I was in an intense training program, where I was constantly pressured, stressed, and exhausted.

Unfortunately, as the early years went by, I didn't learn to soften my expectations much, and my wife grew weary and discouraged. She told me that she finally came to the conclusion that even though she had tried so hard, since it didn't seem to make a difference, why keep trying?

To make a long story short, we both began to grow cold. We developed a certain hopelessness in our marriage, and an overwhelming pain and emptiness entered our home.

After a number of years, I began realizing that a great deal of what had occurred in our marriage was due to my perfectionistic attitude. I wanted to change, but by this time, my wife had grown distant and was filled with resentment. It seemed that now any efforts I made were not enough. I was reaping what I had sown.

Our marriage seemed to be a constant battleground—over almost any issue, big or small. If I felt one way, she looked at it differently. I wanted respect as a husband and leadership in the home; she gave me neither. She wanted unconditional love and cherishing; I gave her neither.

A few years ago, we finally sat down together to try to repair our marriage. We were tired and unhappy. It no longer seemed to matter who was right and who was wrong. We knew, as we had all along, that our marriage wasn't the kind we had hoped to model for our children. Our ministry was limited because of it. But most important, we knew our marriage wasn't pleasing to God. In fact, it seemed in many ways a mockery to God. We committed ourselves to changing. And this time we began to make some progress.

But the one thing that seemed to be consistently missing was joy in our marriage. We went about dutifully fulfilling our marital responsibilities, but there was no joy. But we had lived in pain for so long that we could survive without joy as long as bitterness and anger were no longer the dominating forces.

A few years ago, my wife began living the principles in this book. I am not prone to being overly dramatic, but honestly, she was transformed. She literally became a different person in many areas of her life. Anger was replaced with kindness, pride with humility, and opposition with respect. She developed the sincere desire to serve and respect me as her husband. And she seemed to burn with a desire to serve and obey God in a way that she never had before.

"She took her eyes off of me and put them on Christ, and that is where the change began."

I began seeing a newness in my wife—in the way she talked, in the way she spoke to me, in the way she responded to my requests, in the way she served me, and in the way she humbled herself in an effort to be obedient to God. I was seeing Christ in her. So it was Christ who began changing my wife, and in turn it was Christ in her that softened my own heart.

We still had (and have) our differences, of course, like any married couple. But I saw in my wife a willingness, almost an eagerness, to make things right between herself and God, and as a result, things were made right between us. I'm sure if you asked her, she'd say that lots of times she may not have felt I deserved any special treatment. But there was no doubt in her mind that God did. She took her eyes off of me and put them on Christ, and that is where the change began.

How has this transformation made me feel?

First of all, I feel much more free to be who I am because my wife is no longer constantly judging me. I felt that no matter what I did, I was going to lose. I now feel like I have an advocate rather than an adversary in my wife. And this gives me a confidence I never had before.

I also feel affection for my wife. I know this probably sounds strange, but it's hard to show affection when there's a high likelihood that it will be rejected. Although she always wanted affection, I always had a hard time giving it because of the constant battle between us. Because of our struggles, we poured our affections into our children, and they became our priorities. But now our priorities have become each other, and affection for each other comes more naturally and freely. Our children love this!

I can tell you that all the men I know, including me, desire respect more than love. If a man doesn't feel respected in his home, he not only feels undermined on issues in the home, but also undermined as a man. I now feel respected by my wife. I feel that I am the leader of the home, and my wife's willingness to respect that title causes me to more freely seek her wisdom and counsel. It has also caused me to respect *her* more deeply.

Another thing is that the hypocrisy that plagued me in past years is gone. The guilt at knowing that my personal life was a mess as I tried to maintain various ministries is gone. I no longer feel hindered as I approach God.

I no longer dread coming home from work, wondering what the temperature will be when I walk through the door. For many men (and women too, no doubt) there's a lot of pressure and stress during the workday. Most of us want to come home and feel appreciated and accepted as we are. My wife used to tell me that she didn't worry about my feeling unappreciated because in her eyes I got that affirmation and acceptance at work. But when I experience acceptance at home, I am far better equipped to do well at work.

Fun and friendship have also reentered our marriage. We enjoy each other and often just sit and talk, which we never used to do.

I feel far more peaceful. In the past, even in the good times, we knew that it was just a matter of time before things would deteriorate again. But now, even on our bad days, the foundation remains firm. We have rediscovered how invaluable humility is. It is one of the cornerstones of our marriage.

We have rediscovered how invaluable humility is. It is the cornerstone of our marriage.

Finally, I feel excited—excited by the spiritual journey my wife is taking, excited by the spiritual insights we are gaining from one another, and excited by the spiritual intimacy we are beginning to experience.

If I could leave you with a final thought, it's this: My wife made a decision to honor God through *obedience* and committed to apply biblical principles to our marriage. As a result, God has given us a foundation that was never there before. She didn't focus on me; she focused on God. And the fruits of love, patience, forgiveness, and respect have entered our home.

I humbly share with you today that in our marriage our hope was rediscovered when my wife committed to being obedient to godly principles. That's not to say that I think the responsibility is more the wife's than the husband's, because I don't. We are all responsible for our actions. But I would encourage you not to wait for your husbands. Instead, start doing *now* what you know God has called you to do. I know this may seem hard, but don't wait. God doesn't honor our waiting; He doesn't honor our intentions— but He does honor our obedience.

I'd like to close with some Scripture that seems to capture the essence of these issues:

> Therefore, since we are surrounded by such a great cloud of witnesses, let us throw off everything that hinders and the sin that so easily entangles, and let us run with perseverance the race marked out for us. *Let us fix our eyes on Jesus,* the author and perfecter of our faith, who for the joy set before him endured the cross, scorning its shame, and sat down at the right hand of the throne of God. *Consider him* who endured such opposition from sinful men, so that you will not grow weary and lose heart. (Hebrews 12:1–3)

May each of you reading this book fix your eyes on Jesus and in so doing become who He made you to be.

Epilogue

J ohn 2 tells about a wedding in Cana where the host ran out of wine. Jesus' mother went to Him, knowing He could take care of it. He took water from six large jars and changed it into wine. The wine that had His touch upon it was far better than what had been served originally.

As we individually meditated on this verse, we noticed that Jesus accepted wedding invitations and that when His help was requested, He responded. So in the privacy of our own homes, we invited Him into our marriages, asking Him to fill what we had run out of:

hope...

joy...

desire...

peace...

love....

And He gave His help in overwhelming measure. As we began to follow His plan for us, we experienced His blessings as never before.

There are still days when we fail, but we know to Whom we must turn. We sometimes slip back into questioning: "Did God really say...?" But we know He did! And we don't want to live our lives the old way ever again.

Would you consider inviting Jesus into your marriage? Would you consider putting His Word to work in your life?

In his book *Strike the Original Match,* Charles Swindoll gives this warning:

> Let me mention one more "cheap substitute" so common among Christian wives in our day. It is learning about what's right rather than doing what is right.... It has been my observation that a large percentage of Christian wives know more—much more—than they put into practice. And yet, they are continually interested in attending another class, taking another course, reading another book, going to another seminar.... And what results?

Normally, greater guilt. Or on the other side, an enormous backlog of theoretical data that blinds and thickens the conscience rather than spurs it into action. Learning more truth is a poor and cheap substitute for stopping and putting into action the truth already learned.[1]

Knowledge isn't the answer; obedience is! Never would the ark have been built if Noah hadn't picked up that first piece of wood in obedience to God. Never would the Red Sea have been crossed if Moses hadn't taken that first step to lead his people out of bondage.

We challenge you to take that first step, as politically incorrect as it might seem, and begin a journey that will change your life forever! Remember, you're never alone. There is One traveling with you who never slumbers, sleeps, or grows weary.

It is the dearest thing to place your life in the hands of God, not caring what the world thinks, saying, "Lord, change me." This correct living is called obedience, and your life will never be the same!

Would you consider doing this today?

The publisher and author would love to hear your
comments about this book. *Please contact us at:*
www.multnomah.net

Study
Guide

Chapter 1: Men Need Help

1. Read Genesis 2:15, 18. In the Garden of Eden, what role did God give to man? To woman? Which role seems more task-oriented? Which role seems more relational?

2. Define the word *helper*. How can a woman help her husband? Describe the ways you help your husband.

3. In Genesis 2:16–17, what warning did God give Adam? Was Eve present when God gave Adam this warning?

4. In Genesis 2:18, what does God say about the aloneness of man? Is your husband lonely? How can you help your husband overcome loneliness?

5. In Genesis 2:24, what three things does God say about the marriage relationship? Was the sexual relationship between the man and the woman introduced before or after sin entered the world? How is this significant?

6. What did you learn from this chapter that will impact your life most?

Chapter 2: Choices! Choices! Choices!

1. In Genesis 3:1, what were the first words the serpent used when he began to tempt Eve? When reading or discussing God's Word, have you ever added your own "twist" to what is written about the role of a wife? Do you know your God-given role in this area? If not, are you willing to learn what He has to say…and apply it?

2. In Genesis 3:1–6, Eve made choices that affected both her and her husband. What was the sequence of her choices? As you study this example, what additional steps do you see that you need to take to protect yourself against the enemy (see page 53)?

3. What happens when we focus on what we *can't have* or *don't have* instead of thanking God for what we *do have?* Do you struggle with this? If so, how?

4. How much influence did Eve have over Adam? What kind of influence do you have over your husband? Are you cautious in this matter?

5. What were the consequences of Eve's choices? What do you think women are now prone to do? How is this tendency displayed in your own marriage? See Genesis 3:16.

6. Describe something new you learned from this chapter.

Chapter 3: Let Freedom Ring

1. What is forgiveness? How quick are you to forgive your husband? What does Jesus say about forgiveness (see Matthew 18:21–35)?

2. The parable in Matthew 18:21–35 describes two men who are in prison for the very same offense. What is the offense? Who has the more severe sentence? Why?

3. Read Romans 12:19. Why is it important for us not to take our own revenge? What happens when we leave the matter in God's hands? Name various ways women take revenge against their husbands.

4. Husbands and wives are wired differently. Are differing personality types a source of discord in your marriage? If so, how does this added understanding change your perspective?

5. Read Colossians 2:13–14. How does Jesus' death on the cross relate to the forgiveness of your sins? How do we receive the forgiveness Christ obtained for us at the cross (see page 87)?

6. How has reading this chapter helped you?

Chapter 4: What Makes Your Heart Beat Faster?

1. How can you experience more love, peace, and joy in your marriage (John 14:21, 27; 15:9, 11)?

2. What is your prayer life like? Do you pray regularly for your husband? If you don't, who does?

3. How do you begin your day? For suggestions, see pages 115–117.

4. Read John 15:4–5. What is the outcome of abiding in Christ? What impact would constantly abiding in Him have in your marriage (see pages 109–112)?

5. How would putting these principles into practice impact your marriage? Your relationship with God?

Chapter 5: Who's in Charge Around Here Anyway?

1. What does "Wives, submit to your husbands as to the Lord" (Ephesians 5:22–24) mean to you? Define the word *submission* (see page 131). Look up the word *submission* in both an English dictionary and a Bible dictionary.

2. Does this mean that you should never voice your opinion (see pages 137)?

3. Read 1 Peter 3:1–2. What may happen when a wife submits willingly to her nonbelieving husband?

4. What exceptions are there to submission (see pages 152–153)?

5. Where is submission seen supremely (see 1 Corinthians 11:3)?

6. After reading this chapter, what principle do you understand more clearly?

Chapter 6: Behavior Matters

1. Name some ways for a wife to express respect for her husband. Can you think of more ways you can express respect for your husband?

2. Do you think it is important for a man to know that his wife respects him? Why? How do you think children are impacted when they witness their mother showing respect for their dad?

3. Does your husband want you to listen to him? How important do you think this is to him? Do you think you need to improve your listening skills? What will you begin to do differently?

4. What would your husband say if you asked him if he thinks you honor him? Would your children say that you honor their father? Your friends and family? Is your husband completely confident that you love him?

5. What do you think would happen *to you* if you started focusing on your husband's strengths and stopped focusing on what you deem his faults? What do you think his reaction would be if you began to admire him?

6. Now that you have read this chapter, what will you begin to do differently?

Chapter 7: Who Says Beauty Is Only Skin Deep?

1. Read 1 Peter 3:3 in the *New American Standard Bible* and *Amplified Bible* ("and not let your beauty be merely external..."). How important is your outer beauty to you? To your husband? What practical steps can you take to begin to improve your outward beauty? Also read Proverbs 31:22 and Song of Songs 4:1–10.

2. How important is your inner beauty to you? To your husband? To God? Read 1 Peter 3:4.

3. According to 1 Peter 3:4, a woman who has a gentle and quiet spirit is very precious in the sight of God. What does the word *gentle* mean? How does a woman cultivate a quiet spirit?

4. Practical tips for maintaining a quiet spirit are listed on pages 193–194. Which of these do you need to add to your own maintenance plan?

5. After reviewing this chapter, what actions have you decided to take?

Chapter 8: First Things First

1. Which relationship did God give to Eve first, being a wife or being a mother (see Genesis 2:18–25)?

2. A wife's first priority is her relationship with God. Her first earthly priority is her relationship with her husband. If you asked your husband, would he say that he *knows* he is your first earthly priority? Or would he say that the children are? Your job? Another activity, relationship, or function in your life?

3. How do you think your answer to the above question impacts your husband? You? Your children (see Proverbs 22:6)? Your relationship with God?

4. If you need a major overhaul in this area, how will you begin to restructure your priorities (see pages 226–228)?

5. After reading this chapter, what changes will you make?

Chapter 9: Why Am I Doing This?

1. As a wife, do you now view your role as a joy? As a duty? As a ministry?

2. Read Colossians 3:23–24. If you began to deem your role as a wife as being a ministry to Christ, what would happen? How would this affect your husband? Your children? Your own spiritual walk?

3. Read Matthew 20:26–28. Who best models ministry to others?

4. In Colossians 3:23–24, God promises that those who serve *Him* in their everyday lives will be rewarded with an inheritance from the Lord. What do you think that reward might be in your everyday life? In eternity (see 1 Corinthians 9:25; 1 Thessalonians 2:19; 2 Timothy 4:8; 1 Peter 5:4; Revelations 4:4)?

5. As a result of reading this chapter, what will you do differently?

Notes

Chapter 1

1. Ed Wheat, *Love Life for Every Married Couple* (Grand Rapids, Mich.: Zondervan Publishing House, 1980), 61.

Chapter 2

1. Susan T. Foh, *Women and the Word of God: A Response to Biblical Feminism* (Phillipsburg, N.J.: Presbyterian and Reformed Publishing Co., 1979), 69.
2. *The Billy Graham Christian Worker's Handbook* (Minneapolis, Minn.: Worldwide Publishers, 1984), 5–6.
3. Frank B. Minirth and Paul D. Meier, *Happiness Is a Choice* (Grand Rapids, Mich.: Baker Book House, 1978), 174.

Chapter 3

1. Mels Carbonell, *Discover Your Giftedness in Christ,* Combination Profile 3 Lessons Study Guide. Copyright 1966 by Mels Carbonell, Ph.D.

Chapter 4

1. A. W. Tozer, *The Pursuit of God* (Old Tappan, N.J.: Fleming H. Revel, 1982), 126.
2. W. Glyn Evans, *Daily with the King* (Chicago, Ill.: Moody Press, 1979), 249.
3. Andrew Murray, cited in Warren and Ruth Myers, *31 Days of Prayer* (Sisters, Ore.: Questar Publishers, Inc., 1997), 159.
4. Myers, *31 Days of Prayer,* 42.

5. V. Raymond Edman, *They Found the Secret* (Grand Rapids, Mich.: Zondervan, 1984), 19.

6. Myers, *31 Days of Prayer,* 158.

7. A. Wetherell Johnson, Bible Study Fellowship notes.

Chapter 5

1. Paraphrased from *The Life Application Bible—The Living Bible* (Wheaton, Ill.: Tyndale House, 1988), 1934.

2. Dr. James C. Dobson, *Straight Talk* (Dallas, Tex.: Word Publishing, 1991), 100–1.

3. John F. Walvoord and Roy B. Zuck, *The Bible Knowledge Commentary* (Wheaton, Ill.: Victor Books, 1983), 683.

Chapter 6

1. 1 Peter 2 (AMP).

2. *New Webster's Dictionary and Thesaurus of the English Language* (Danbury, Conn.: Lexicon Publications, Inc., 1993), 848.

3. Ibid., 252.

4. Ibid., 851.

5. Ibid., 579.

6. Ibid., 58.

7. Ibid., 57.

8. Ibid., 923.

9. Ibid., 707.

10. Ibid., 413.

Chapter 7

1. *New Webster's Dictionary and Thesaurus of the English Language* (Danbury, Conn.: Lexicon Publications, Inc., 1993), 511.

2. Ibid., 581.

Chapter 9

1. Lawrence J. Crabb Jr., *The Marriage Builder* (Grand Rapids, Mich.: Zondervan Publishing House, 1982), 58–9.

Epilogue

1. Charles R. Swindoll, *Strike the Original Match* (Portland, Ore.: Multnomah Press, 1980), 59.

HELP!
I DON'T SPEAK TEENAGER!

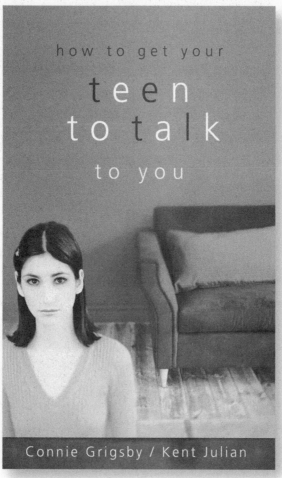

how to get your

teen
to talk

to you

Connie Grigsby / Kent Julian

Cover Not Final

Communication between parents and teens is at an all-time low. Besides marriage, this is the area where adults seem to struggle most. This user-friendly book will help readers get inside their teen's mind, showing them what turns today's teen on and off in terms of communication. Topics include: Ten Best Ways to Kill a Conversation, Language Barriers, Don't Be Afraid to Say No, and Gender Differences and Communication.

ISBN 1-59052-064-5

SPEAK YOUR HUSBAND'S LANGUAGE: MALE!

Nancy Cobb and Connie Grigsby, both popular teachers and speakers and co-authors of *The Politically Incorrect Wife* have collaborated on a primer that promises to resolve the age-old mystery of communication between the sexes -and leave men and women conversing happily. This fun, practical, and life-changing book will keep you alternating between laughter and tears as you discover simple ways to:

- Cultivate a sense of humor about your male and female differences.
- Open conversations with your mate, and keep them going.
- Frame what you are saying within masculine interest areas.
- Respond proactively to what your husband shares-promoting more sharing.

ISBN 1-57673-771-3